THE DALAI LAMA

Recent Titles in Greenwood Biographies

J.K. Rowling: A Biography
Connie Ann Kirk

THE DALAI LAMA

A Biography

Patricia Cronin Marcello

GREENWOOD BIOGRAPHIES

GREENWOOD PRESS
WESTPORT, CONNECTICUT · LONDON

Library of Congress Cataloging-in-Publication Data

Marcello, Patricia M.
  The Dalai Lama : a biography / Patricia Cronin Marcello.
    p. cm.—(Greenwood biographies series, ISSN 1540–4900)
  Includes bibliographical references and index.
  ISBN 0–313–32207–4 (alk. paper)
  1. Bstan-'dzin-rgya-mtsho, Dalai Lama XIV, 1935– 2. Dalai Lamas—Biography. I.
Title. II. Series.
BQ7935.B777 M37   2003
294.3'923'092—dc21   2002075338
[B]

British Library Cataloguing in Publication Data is available.

Library of Congress Catalog Card Number: 2002075338
ISBN: 0–313–32207–4
ISSN: 1540–4900

First published in 2003

Greenwood Press, 88 Post Road West, Westport, CT 06881
An imprint of Greenwood Publishing Group, Inc.
www.greenwood.com

Printed in the United States of America

∞

The paper used in this book complies with the
Permanent Paper Standard issued by the National
Information Standards Organization (Z39.48–1984).

10 9 8 7 6 5 4 3 2 1

294.392 MAR 2003

For Vince and Dorothy, who live through me; for Barbara, who taught me to read; and most of all, for my beloved Patrick and Shannon, my continued sources of support. Also for Sal and Burt and Dottie for taking the time to describe the essence of Tibet.

CONTENTS

Photo essay follows page 77.

SERIES FOREWORD

In response to high school and public library needs, Greenwood developed this distinguished series of full-length biographies specifically for student use. Prepared by field experts and professionals, these engaging biographies are tailored for high school students who need challenging yet accessible biographies. Ideal for secondary school assignments, the length, format, and subject areas are designed to meet educators' requirements and students' interests.

Greenwood offers an extensive selection of biographies spanning all curriculum related subject areas including social studies, the sciences, literature and the arts, history and politics, as well as popular culture, covering public figures and famous personalities from all time periods and backgrounds, both historic and contemporary, who have made an impact on American and/or world culture. Greenwood biographies were chosen based on comprehensive feedback from librarians and educators. Consideration was given to both curriculum relevance and inherent interest. The result is an intriguing mix of the well known and the unexpected, the saints and sinners from long-ago history and contemporary pop culture. Readers will find a wide array of subject choices from fascinating crime figures like Al Capone to inspiring pioneers like Margaret Mead, from the greatest minds of our time like Stephen Hawking to the most amazing success stories of our day like J.K. Rowling.

While the emphasis is on fact, not glorification, the books are meant to be fun to read. Each volume provides in-depth information about the subject's life from birth through childhood, the teen years, and adulthood. A thorough account relates family background and education, traces personal and professional influences, and explores struggles, accomplishments, and contributions. A timeline highlights the most significant life events against a historical perspective. Suggestions for further reading give the biographies added reference value.

INTRODUCTION

In 1959, the twenty-four-year-old Dalai Lama escaped communist rule in his native Tibet, the "Shangri-la" of lore. Situated high in the Himalayan Mountains, Tibet is a land of thin oxygen, chilling temperatures, and sparse vegetation. Tibet is also a land of ritual, seated in the Buddhist religion.

The Dalai Lama had lived in strict seclusion in Tibet from the time he was two years old and had communicated only with his immediate family members and close personal servants. As Dalai Lama, tradition kept him a virtual prisoner, until violence drove him from the country for the sake of his people. Tibetans believe that without the Dalai Lama, there could be no Tibet.

The Dalai Lama has found personal and intellectual freedom at his temporary home in India since 1959, and has organized a new, highly developed government-in-exile. This democratic system is poised to reassume control in a Tibet that is free to oversee its own government and to pursue Buddhism, the guiding force for all events in everyday Tibetan life.

As the Dalai Lama travels from country to country, seeking support for the Tibet he envisions, the 1989 Nobel Peace Prize winner has become a worldwide celebrity. As an emissary of compassion, he spreads the spirit of Buddhism and has attracted many high-profile followers to his cause and his religion, although he has never sought converts. His charm and charisma draw people, who see this peer to the pope or the archbishop of Canterbury as a highly intelligent, warm, and open individual. Yet most who are drawn to him have little idea how far from traditional Tibetan protocol he has drifted.

Because the Dalai Lama is considered not only a god-king by all Tibetans but also the heart and soul of Tibet, most of his life must be examined via an objective look at Tibetan history from ancient times. Only through Tibet can the role of Dalai Lama be fully understood.

In pursuit of this examination, four main sources have provided the information for this book: books, magazine and newspaper articles, governmental documents and correspondence, and personal interviews with recent visitors to Tibet.

Much of the foreign and governmental documents, communiqués, and articles were retrieved online from various sources, of which the URLs are listed in the notes and bibliography.

TIMELINE OF EVENTS IN THE LIFE OF THE FOURTEENTH DALAI LAMA

July 6, 1935	Birth of Lhamo Dhondup, the future Dalai Lama
July 21, 1939	Leaves Amdo for Lhasa
February 22, 1940	Installed on Lion Throne and becomes Fourteenth Dalai Lama of Tibet
January 15, 1946	Heinrich Harrer and Peter Aufschnaiter arrive in Lhasa
1947	Death of father, Choekyong Tsering
1948	Formally admitted to Ganden, Drepung, and Sera monasteries
January 1, 1950	Communists announce plans to "liberate" Tibet
August 15, 1950	Earthquake of 8.6 magnitude strikes Assam, and rattles Tibet
October 7, 1950	China's People's Liberation Army invades Kham
November 17, 1950	Assumes temporal control of Tibet
December 19, 1950	Heads for Yadong, near Indian border, to escape Chinese invaders, and sends treasure boxes to Sikkim
January 4, 1951	Reaches Yadong
May 23, 1951	The Seventeen-Point Agreement is signed in Beijing by representatives without authority
June 1951	Learns of Seventeen-Point Agreement on Radio Beijing
August 18, 1951	Returns to Lhasa to work out a relationship with the Chinese

May 22, 1952	Under Chinese pressure, asks prime ministers to resign
July 11, 1954	Leaves Lhasa for Beijing
September 5, 1954	Arrives in Beijing with Panchen Lama
September 12, 1954	Welcomed by Mao Zedong
June 29, 1955	Returns to Lhasa after touring China
April 22, 1956	Preparatory Committee for the Autonomous Region of Tibet (PCART) opens at Lhasa Hall; Dalai Lama declared chairman
October 1, 1956	Nehru wires Beijing asking permission for Dalai Lama and Panchen Lama to attend Buddha Jayanti in India
November 12, 1956	Leaves Tibet to attend Buddha Jayanti in India with Panchen Lama
April 1, 1957	Returns from India
July 4, 1957	"Golden Throne" dedication
March 1, 1959	Invited to attend dance performance at Chinese camp; passes final exams for doctorate in metaphysics
March 4, 1959	Asked again to attend dance performance and agrees to go on March 10
March 10, 1959	Cancels attendance at performance as Tibetan citizens surround the Norbulingka
March 17, 1959	Dalai Lama, his family, and his close advisors leave Lhasa
March 20, 1959	Chinese bomb Norbulingka
March 30, 1959	Crosses the Indian border
April 19, 1959	Sets off for Mussoorie, India, to live in exile at Birla House
June 20, 1959	Testifies before International Commission of Jurists
April 29, 1960	Leaves for new home in Dharamsala, India
1962	*My Land and My People*, the autobiography of the Dalai Lama, is published
November 1964	Tsering Dolma, Dalai Lama's sister, dies
September 25, 1967	Sets off for visits to Japan and Thailand
1968	Father Thomas Merton visits Dalai Lama in India
September 29, 1973	Arrives in Rome for a six-week tour of Europe and Scandinavia; meets Pope Paul VI
1980	Meets Pope John Paul II
January 12, 1981	Diki Tsering, Dalai Lama's mother, dies
1982	Lobsang Samten, Dalai Lama's brother, dies

February 28, 1987	Receives Albert Schweitzer Humanitarian Award
July 21, 1989	Receives Raoul Wallenberg Human Rights Award
December 10, 1989	Accepts Nobel Peace Prize
1990	*Freedom in Exile: The Autobiography of the Dalai Lama* is published
February 2, 1990	Meets Vaclav Havel, President of Czechoslovakia
April 16, 1991	Meets U.S. President George Bush; first meeting of Dalai Lama and U.S. president
April 24, 1994	Meets U.S. President Bill Clinton and Vice President Al Gore
April 27, 1994	Receives doctorate in human arts and letters from Columbia University
July 1994	Chinese ban all photographs of the Dalai Lama from government offices
May 14, 1995	Proclaims Eleventh Panchen Lama
June 16, 1995	Accuses China of kidnapping his choice for Panchen Lama
December 1997	*Kundun* and *Seven Years in Tibet* released in the United States
December 26, 1997	Arts and Entertainment network airs *The Dalai Lama: The Soul of Tibet*
April 28, 1998	Admits failure of "middle way" in dealings with China
May 13, 1998	Addresses Wisconsin State Assembly
April 5, 1999	Leaves for visit to South America
November 24, 1999	Life Achievement Award, Hadassah Women's Zionist Organization
August 24, 2000	Barred from Millennium World Peace Summit at United Nations due to Chinese pressure
December 4, 2000	Celebrates fifty years as Tibetan head of state
May 2001	Visits six U.S. cities: Madison, WI; Los Angeles; San Francisco; San Jose; Salt Lake City; and Minneapolis
May 23, 2001	Meets U.S. President George W. Bush and U.S. Secretary of State Colin Powell at the White House

Chapter 1

THE BIRTH OF LHAMO DHONDUP

In a cold, unyielding province, high in northeastern Tibet, the future Fourteenth Dalai Lama, Lhamo Dhondup, was born on a straw-covered dirt floor on July 6, 1935. His introduction to the world was as mundane as baking bread, although his future was to be as important to Tibet as Christ was to Christmas. To the Tibetan people, the Dalai Lama was not only the embodiment of a living god but also Tibet itself. From that July day forward, the country's future, its spiritual strength, and its people rested in his tiny, yet undiscovered, hands.

The name Lhamo Dhonup meant "wish-fulfilling goddess," and as with all Tibetan names, it was unlike those of Western custom, which bear a forename and a surname. In Tibet, only the full essence of the name is significant. In keeping with Tibetan custom, his birth garnered no special attention. He was just another boy born to peasant parents, probably destined for life in a monastery, as was the fate of many other boys born during that time in that particular place.

Even his immediate family was unaware of his birth when it happened, as his mother had simply walked into the barn to deliver him. Most family members would recognize the child only by his cries, or as another mouth at the dinner table, but as time progressed, neighbors would learn of his arrival and bestow small gifts of clothes, blankets, and bread upon him. By these tokens, he was no more extraordinary than any other child born in the village of Takster, and his roots were no nobler.

A MOTHER'S JOURNEY

Diki Tsering, Lhamo Dhondup's mother, was born with the name Sonam Tsomo in the village of Churka, within the eastern province of Amdo in historic Tibet, around 1901. At the age of five, her family immigrated to Guyahu, also in Amdo, to a large farm. As there was no formal education for girls at that time in Tibet, she immediately began to learn domestic duties and to pray, and was taught that her future existed only in a life of marriage and hard work. As a Buddhist, she learned that the road to a full and self-contained life lay in suffering, and she embraced these tenets.

Tibetan parents were very protective of young girls. Diki Tsering's parents kept her very close to home and rarely permitted her to leave the terrace or garden. By age seven, in addition to tending to her personal cleanliness, she was expected to brew tea and to bake bread for the entire family—although to achieve these culinary tasks, she required a chair to reach the cooking surface.

At thirteen, as Tibetan custom dictated, her family arranged her marriage to Choekyong Tsering. Although the bridegroom's family wanted an immediate union, the girl's family insisted that she would not be wed until she was sixteen years old. When that year arrived, astrologers set the wedding date—just as they set all dates of important events in Tibetan culture, which is highly structured with deep roots in spirituality and Tibetan myth. Many traditions pertain to the occasion of marriage.

Just before the wedding, Diki Tsering's in-laws presented her with a trousseau, as it was customary for the bride to wear only clothes handmade by the bridegroom's family from her nuptials onward. On the day of her departure for her husband's home, her mother burned her old wardrobe and ritually wailed into the flames in anguish over losing her daughter.

Sonam Tsomo's journey consisted of a treacherous nine-hour trek on horseback to Choekyong Tsering's family farm in Takster, Amdo. On the day of her arrival, she was presented with a white ceremonial scarf (*kata*), given as a gesture of respect, but did not see her groom. She was fed and entertained by a great deal of ceremonial singing, but two more days would pass before she actually met her prospective husband. On that day, Sonam Tsomo's name changed to Diki Tsering, meaning "ocean of luck."

A FAMILY BEGINS TO SHOW PROMISE

The life of a new daughter-in-law was rigorous in historic Tibet, sometimes requiring twenty hours of work each day. Like many other Tibetan daughters-in-law, Diki Tsering was abused by her mother-in-law, both physically and emotionally, and was expected to perform most of the menial labor in the household and around the crop and livestock farm. After a few years of hard labor, Diki Tsering's position improved in the family, and eventually, when her in-laws retired, she inherited control of the household.

Strong of character in his straightforwardness and honesty, Choekyong Tsering always enjoyed a good time. He had a quick temper but was also kind and never held grudges. He loved gambling and riding fast horses, which he also knew how to doctor, but he rarely worked in the fields. As Diki Tsering became mistress of the household with his parents' passing, Choekyong Tsering became master of the fields.

The couple had four children by the time Lhamo Dhondup was born— Tsering Dolma, born in 1919; Thubten Jigme Norbu, born in 1922; Gyalo Thondup, born in 1928; and Lobsang Samten, born in 1933. Two more children would be born after Lhamo Dhondup: Jetsun Pema in 1940 and Tendzin Choegyal in 1946. Though Diki Tsering bore a total of sixteen children during her life, only seven would survive past infancy.

Long before the family learned of Lhamo Dhondup's destiny, fate honored another child in the family. His eldest brother, Thubten Jigme Norbu, was elevated to a higher station by the Thirteenth Dalai Lama, Thubten Gyatso, the spiritual and political leader of Tibet at that time. Although Thubten Jigme Norbu's influence would not be as extensive as his yet-to-be-born brother's, his position was still well revered by the Tibetan people.

This tribute came to the boy when he was proclaimed the rebirth of the previous high lama from the local monastery. Reincarnation is a central principle of the Buddhist religion, and Tibetans are overwhelmingly Buddhist. They believe that the soul receives corporeal life repeatedly, until a state of enlightenment, or Buddhahood, is reached. A spirit who can choose the time and place of its reincarnation is known as a *tulku*, or an incarnate lama, which means "living teacher." Tulkus are often bestowed with the title Rinpoché, which means "precious one," and many of them are monks, who are said to leave signs leading to the discovery of their next incarnation. Only the Dalai Lama can proclaim a tulku.

The previous Takster Rinpoché was Choekyong Tsering's maternal uncle, who headed the monastery at Kumbum, close to the village of Takster. Kumbum, which means "palace of a thousand images," was the most important monastery in the Amdo region. Built around 1440, the center was a memorial to the birthplace of Tsonkapa, the founder of Tibet's largest Buddhist sect, the Gelugpas, or "Followers of the virtuous way."

When the old Takster Rinpoché died, Choekyong Tsering's mother wished for Diki Tsering to have a male child, hoping he would be the reincarnation of her dead brother, but was furious when her son's first child proved to be a girl. The Dalai Lama's advisors found another baby they thought to be the incarnate lama, but the child died before he was a year old. For reasons unclear to all but the Thirteenth Dalai Lama, he had been hesitant to name this first baby successor to Takster Rinpoché, and when the boy died, everyone accepted the Dalai Lama's lack of action as prescience. When Thubten Jigme Norbu was born, his grandmother was elated, and shortly after his first birthday, the Thirteenth Dalai Lama sent a letter to his parents, naming the child Takster Rinpoché and declaring him the reincarnation of the dead abbot. He was soon sent to Kumbum to begin a monastic life.

STRONG INFLUENCES, HUMBLE HOME

Early religious training was customary in Tibet in the early 1920s. Although large families were the norm, parents were often too poor to support them, so they typically sent at least one boy to a monastery. Although the practice was uncommon in outlying districts, in the city of Lhasa— the Tibetan capital—parents of large families often sent girls to nunneries. In these cloisters, children not only received clothing and shelter, but also were trained in reading, writing, and the Buddhist Dharma, or the holy teachings of Buddha.

Boys who stayed at home worked in the fields with their fathers and learned farming and animal husbandry. Girls continued to practice household duties and prepared for marriage. In old Tibet, the birth of a girl was considered a hardship or even a curse, because girls did nothing to aid production; they only consumed. In poor families, girls were frequently drowned immediately after birth.

This disregard for the sanctity of life comes from a standard fare of intense hardship and pervasive death. Once, due to a terrible famine in neighboring China, two beggars appeared at Choekyong Tsering's farmhouse door, carrying the body of their dead baby. Diki Tsering offered them food and asked whether they would like help with its burial. When she realized they had no intention of burying the child but intended to eat it instead, Diki Tsering immediately emptied the contents of the household stores and gave all the family's provisions to the couple. This quality of compassion would carry through to little Lhamo Dhondup, who would learn of his great destiny as the incarnation of the god of compassion in years to come.

The boy began his life in eastern Tibet, on the frontier with China. Situated on a caravan trail, Takster began as a nomadic village of black tents, made from the hair of yaks—wild, shaggy-haired oxen, indigenous to the mountain regions of central Asia. A stream flowed nearby the village, and nomads found healthy pastures where they could farm barley, oats, and vegetables, and they made a permanent settlement. By 1935, Takster was a village of about thirty houses.

In each of these houses, Buddhism was the practiced religion, and in Tibet, Buddhists follow the Mahayana school. This group aims to attain the highest stage of Nirvana, or liberation from bondage of the human form. They seek to eradicate sin and delusion, which are negative karmas (causes and effects), and to attain Buddhahood, which comes to all sentient beings through several lives of service.

Each Buddhist household contains an altar with an image of the Buddha, some scripture, and a stupa or *chorten*. These domed monuments can be large or, in the case of a household altar, small, and may hold relics of departed lamas. Flowers and butter lamps (small bowls that hold yak butter and a wick) surround the family's daily offering to the Buddha. Altars are present in cities and towns, palaces and farms, and all serve the same purpose of reducing mental stress and obtaining guidance.

The farm belonging to Lhamo Dhondup's family was small, and though they were not peasants, neither were they wealthy nobles. They grew barley and buckwheat, which were the main crops throughout Tibet at that time, as well as potatoes. Irrigation was nonexistent, and farmers depended upon rainwater to irrigate their crops, which were often lost to drought or hailstorms. Life was hard, but following the old Buddhist traditions of lifelong hardship, for most Amdowas (the people of Amdo), a strong family and a roof over their heads were blessings enough.

Choekyong Tsering's family farmhouse sat in the middle of a group of three homes on the side of a hill, slightly away from the village of Takster. Built of stone and mud, the single-story house was surrounded by a stone wall, with a gate that was shut at night for security. The farmhouse's flat roof was lined with turquoise tiles, and it had unusual gutters of gouged-out juniper wood to channel rainwater into the courtyard. The front of the house was a windowless wall with a single wooden door, decorated with tridents and dragons. In the adjacent courtyard stood a lone tree and a thirty-foot flagpole holding a ten-foot-high white prayer flag, covered with many written prayers. (Buddhists believe that each time a prayer flag flaps in the wind, its prayers are sent to heaven.) Except for one small black-and-white dog and a large Tibetan mastiff, no animals were permitted in this courtyard.

Inside the house, Choekyong Tsering had lined the door with sheepskin to keep it quiet when it opened and closed. Directly through the entrance was the kitchen, where the family spent most of their time; and in the ceiling, beams supported a terra-cotta water tank that was glazed green. At the northern end of the house were the adults' bedroom and a prayer or altar room. To the west were a cowshed, a storeroom, and a guest room. At the southern end lay the stables, where eight cows, chickens, sheep, goats, horses, and yaks, were kept, in addition to seven animals (or *dzomos*) crossbred from yaks and cows. Diki Tsering milked the dzomos and often favored little Lhamo Dhondup with a bowl of warm milk. Before he was two, he was made responsible for collecting eggs from the hen-house.

Living quarters were sparsely furnished, except for some brightly colored cabinets and an area for sleeping, called a *kang*, in each bedroom. Usually made of clay brick, kangs were hollow, raised platforms, which were filled with dried grass and sand, or manure and wood, and lit for warmth. Over the kang, one or more carpets and bedclothes were placed for comfort.

In his early years, Lhamo Dhondup slept on such a kang with his mother. Later, he slept with his siblings in the kitchen near the stove, on the planked wooden floor. All interior rooms had this type of floor, except the non–living space in the kitchen, which had an earthen floor. Flat stone paved the corridor between the rooms as well as the courtyard.

TIBETAN DAILY LIFE

The family's farm normally produced only enough food to sustain them, and they did most of the work, with the help of five regular workers, known as the *yuleg*. During sowing and harvesting season, fifteen to forty more workers, known as the *nyohog*, were hired. Choekyong Tsering oversaw them all, and though Diki Tsering also worked in the fields, she was in charge of the house and the children.

When a surplus of goods from their labors accumulated, Choekyong Tsering exchanged the extra crops for tea, sugar, cotton cloth, and other goods not produced by the farm. This barter system was a way of life in outlying regions of Tibet, and even passing nomads or people in nearby towns traded their horses for grain. Choekyong Tsering was widely known for his ability to select and rear fine horses.

After a strenuous day of farm labor, the family settled in for a meal of roasted barley meal, or *tsampa*, which continues as a staple in the Tibetan diet. Combined with a liquid—usually yak butter tea or a Tibetan beer, *chang*—tsampa is rolled into small balls with the fingers for consumption; it can also be eaten as a powder. Eating tsampa, although an everyday act for a Tibetan, can be rather daunting. One non-Tibetan commented, "Tsampa is an extremely fine powder of roasted barley that when put in the mouth instantly absorbs all the moisture, forcing you to drink something immediately. I found it impossible to eat with my fingers without getting it all over the place."[1] By adding meat and vegetables, tsampa also makes a fine stew.

Yak butter tea is the Tibetan national beverage, and an average Tibetan may drink up to sixty small cups per day for nourishment and hydration, which is of utmost importance in the high altitudes of Tibet. To prepare the tea, butter—made from the milk of yaks—is mixed with strong black tea leaves and salt, and churned until thoroughly blended. Because the leaves are scraped from a compressed block of tea, a bit of yak dung is sometimes added to bind the tiny particles together. A recent visitor to Tibet described the drink this way: "Yak butter tea is more like chicken broth (due to oils from the yak butter) than tea. The flavor is sort of musky."[2]

Tsampa and yak butter tea are served with every meal, and considered the traditional Tibetan foods, along with meat dumplings (*momos*) and a soup made with thick millet noodles (*thukpa*). Tibetans eat two daily meals, and when meat is served at the late meal, it is either mutton or yak flesh, which peasants sometimes eat raw. Fish and foul are considered too filthy to eat, and vegetables—aside from potatoes—are scarce, due to poor growing conditions. Unlike Western diets, the Tibetan diet completely lacks sweets.

Tibetan traditional dress is contrary to Western norms as well. Kimono-like robes, called *chubas*, were once worn by all family members, and along with more modern clothing, they are still used in various forms today. "[Chubas are] caught in at the waist with a broad belt of cloth, woven of various colored threads with red predominant. These cloaks are of sheepskin or of woolen cloth or of silk," wrote Tibetan author Rinchen Lhamo. "The cloak may be worn long or short simply by adjusting it at the belt. Women wear it down to the ankle, men to just above the knee."[3] In winter, chubas are often lined with fur and heavily padded with cotton for warmth. While women wear brightly colored aprons over their chubas in Lhasa, this also varies by region. Inside the chuba, embroidered shirts of cotton or silk accompany trousers of the same material, although men sometimes wear sheepskin pants.

Footwear varies by region. Although both men and women wear knee-high boots, the color and style are different in each province. These boots have flat, yak-leather soles and rise to the knee. Made from felt, cloth, or leather, they are slit at the back, to allow easily access, and are tied at the top with a colored garter.

Jewelry is not merely accessory but a necessary part of a woman's outfit throughout Tibet. Traditionally, women wore rings on every finger and had two piercings in each ear up to an eighth of an inch in diameter, for heavy earrings of gold or silver. They sometimes wore four or five necklaces at once, embellished with coral or turquoise. Because Tibet is so far from the sea, shells were also highly prized as accessory decorations.

As with clothing, the spoken Tibetan language is diverse in dialect. Written Tibetan has its own distinct alphabet, and was solely a spoken language until a written script, based on the Sanskrit handwriting of India, was devised in the seventh century. Because many Tibetan characters cannot immediately be translated into English, Western spellings of Tibetan words often differ. The Dalai Lama says he does not remember most of his early life in Takster. His first memory involves a camel and the communal toilet. "In middle of my sort of 'engagement,'" he told CNN in self-taught English, "one big camel approaching and I run away." He laughs and says it interrupted his "heavy work" there.[4]

This story is indicative of his easy, warm nature. The spirit of his birth name—Lhamo Dhondup or "wish-fulfilling goddess"—seems to flow through his life, as the embodiment of the god of compassion. Many signs arose in connection with his birth, which indicated that he was destined for a greater purpose.

INDICATORS OF A DALAI LAMA'S STATION

Lhamo Dhondup's family had experienced a particularly rough period just before his arrival. First, all thirteen of the family's horses contracted a fatal contagious illness, which was a devastating personal and financial loss. Then, rather than nurturing rain, only hail fell, which destroyed their crops, bringing on a famine that lasted for three years. Lhamo Dhondup's family remained in Takster although many families migrated to other parts of Tibet. Through the goodness of the monks at Kumbum monastery, who gave them lentils, rice, and peas, the family survived the crisis.

Two months before Lhamo Dhondup's birth, Choekyong Tsering fell victim to a mysterious vertigo, which caused him to lose consciousness each time he tried to stand. Yet when Diki Tsering returned to the house after birthing Lhamo Dhondup, her husband was out of bed, apparently cured completely of his puzzling malady. When she told him that she had borne a son, Choekyong Tsering was elated, saying he was no ordinary boy, and a decision to send the infant to a monastery was made immediately.

Soon, a pair of crows came to perch on the roof of the farmhouse. Buddhists believe that crows are the manifestation of the protective deity Maha Kali, or the Great Black One, and the birds have been associated with the births of several other Dalai Lamas. When the nomad settlement of the First Dalai Lama, Gedun Drub, was overrun with marauders, his parents had no means of taking all their children with them quickly, along with enough food to survive. His mother hid the newborn, and returned the next day to find him safely guarded by a large, black crow. Crows were also associated with the births of the Seventh, Eighth, and Twelfth Dalai Lamas. After Lhamo Dhondup was named Dalai Lama, the appearance of the crows on his rooftop was deemed a certain sign of his station in life.

Other incidents in the toddler's life seem to point in the same direction. "He was always packing his clothes and his little belongings," Diki Tsering wrote. "When I asked what he was doing, he would reply that he was packing to go to Lhasa and would take all of us with him."[5]

She also recounts his remarkable particularities, such as never allowing anyone to handle his teacups except her. He disliked quarrelsome people, and before he was two years old, he tried to beat the offenders with sticks. He also disliked smoking, and flew into rages if anyone lit up. The Dalai Lama's family regarded his imperious behavior as a sign that he was destined for great things.

And so he was. But, the little boy's journey had not yet begun. In Lhasa, his great destiny was only preparing to find him.

NOTES

1. Peter Snow Cao, "Lebrang Monastery," *Spoke Notes*, Bike China Adventures, www.bikechina.com/spoke98.htm, 1999.

2. Sal Towse, interview by author, self@towse.com, 2 January 2002.

3. Rinchen Lhamo, *We Tibetans* (Philadelphia: J.B. Lippincott, 1926), p. 89.

4. Quoted in John Christensen, "The Dalai Lama: Man of Peace Takes His Place on World Stage," *CNN Interactive, CNN In-depth Specials—Visions of China—Profiles: The Dalai Lama*, 1999, www.cnn.com/SPECIALS/1999/china.50/inside.china/profiles/dalai.lama.

5. Diki Tsering, *Dalai Lama, My Son. A Mother's Story* (New York: Penguin, 2000), p. 89.

Chapter 2

SEARCH FOR A FOURTEENTH RULER

Before the birth of Lhamo Dhondup, Tibetan people had called Dalai Lama Thubten Gyatso "the Great Thirteenth." He improved ethical standards in matters such as the curtailment of officials borrowing from the government for their private businesses, the reformation of Tibet's feudal legal system, and the abolition of the death penalty. He also made policy that created economic surplus and worked toward the establishment of a British-style army to help make the country secure from Chinese invasions. His reign began in 1895, and he was the first Dalai Lama to assume the complete responsibility of political and spiritual leader since 1758. The Ninth, Tenth, Eleventh, and Twelfth Dalai Lamas all died before reaching maturity.

Many historians suspect that these lamas met their demise at the hands of the Chinese, who—since the early eighteenth century—held suzerainty, or control, over Tibetan international affairs, while Tibet maintained domestic sovereignty. Interregnum governments were more easily controlled than Dalai Lamas, and China had often used the suzerain arrangement to its own advantage up to that time. Although Tibetans continued to view their land as a separate country, China often interfered in Tibet's domestic affairs; though Tibetans disapproved of China's intervention, they needed Chinese military protection. This tenuous alliance held until the early part of the twentieth century.

At that time, the "Great Game" was afoot, when Russia and Great Britain jockeyed for Asian territory in their bids for world domination. Part of that struggle was purported to include dominion over Tibet, which, of course, included the interests of China. Historical thinking on this idea has changed in recent times. Although Russia and Great Britain were undoubtedly rivals in expanding their domains, Russia's only intent regarding Tibet seemed to be the desire to keep it out of Great Britain's hands. Great Britain was more interested in promoting an independent Tibet to buffer their colony of India, which bordered China. The Chinese, however, had always been interested in Tibet, seeing the country as an extension of China's land base where excess population might be shuttled. Tibet was also rich in gold, although at Himalayan heights, mining it would be a difficult extraction.

Due to these circumstances, the Thirteenth Dalai Lama saw a need for protection from imperial Britain and sensed the time was ripe for complete freedom from the Chinese.

China had lost wars with both Great Britain and Japan in the late nineteenth century. Spurred by resentment against these defeats, Chinese nationals revolted against all foreigners living in China during the Boxer Rebellion in 1900. Once again, China lost the battle and was forced to pay indemnities, offer commercial concessions, and suffer foreign troops on Chinese soil. This last defeat accelerated revolution against the Qing dynasty, rulers of China at that time.

The Dalai Lama believed that in light of the developments in China, the suzerains could no longer hold sway over Tibet, or in the event of attack, protect them. Still in his twenties, he was ready to promote Tibetan assertiveness, modernization, and eventual independence.

In his pursuit of a new militaristic patron, the Dalai Lama sent envoys to Europe to evaluate global conditions. Among the party was Agvan Dorjiev, a Buddhist Mongol from the Buriat territory of Russia. He studied at Drepung Monastery in Tibet during the 1870s and later became one of the young Dalai Lama's teachers. The 1901 "Tibetan" expedition to Russia, including Dorjiev and a meeting with Tsar Nicholas II, was well publicized in the Russian press, which disturbed Great Britain.

LOSING BATTLES

Due to Russia's invasion and successful takeover of Central Asia in the last half of the nineteenth century, the British feared encirclement and confrontation in India if the Russians agreed to the patronage of Tibet. The British also saw opportunity. Colonel Sir Thomas H. Holdich wrote, "Tibet is rich in gold—and it is impossible to suppose that the exceptional position which the great highland country occupies in that respect is altogether absent from the minds of those who would grasp at political influence in Lhasa. Tibet is not only rich in the ordinary acceptance of the term; she must be enormously rich—possibly richer than any country in the world."[1]

In 1903, due to the supposed alliance between Tibet and Russia, the British took action. A military expedition, headed by Colonel Francis Younghusband, marched into Khampa Dzong,[2] just inside the Tibetan border, with an escort of two hundred men. However, the Tibetans did little in response, sending low-ranking officials to meet with the colonel and simply asked the British to withdraw.

By January 1904, after making no progress on diplomatic fronts, the British decided to press forward, north to Gyantse, backed by three thousand men bearing arms. While the British readied to march, a Tibetan force was assembling at Tuna, fifty miles inside their border. Upon seeing the Tibetans' lack of modern military equipment, Younghusband tried several times to discuss the situation with the Tibetan general. His compromises were only met with the same demand: that he return to British territory. The Tibetans far outnumbered the British, but their primitive weapons—a few old rifles and swords—were no match for modern British guns. Younghusband declared that he would not fire unless attacked.

The British claim that the first shot fired was Tibetan, followed by a fierce onslaught of many men wielding swords. When smoke from British guns cleared, more than three hundred Tibetans lay dead and many more were wounded. The British then moved on to Gyantse, and later, after two more encounters with Tibetan troops, to the capital of Lhasa. Another 480 Tibetans were killed, although Younghusband continued his pattern of asking for Tibetan surrender, without result.

The Dalai Lama fled Tibet and traveled to Mongolia, as he feared capture by the British. This pushed his regent and other officials to act on his behalf. Though the Tibetans had lost many men and were unable to stop this small British force from invading their territory, Younghusband's fairness and honesty impressed the Tibetans, and relations were soon restored between the two countries. The Anglo-Tibetan trade agreement, signed on September 7, 1904, included concessions in land and money, the right of the British to open trade marts, and Tibet's agreement to exclude other foreign powers from exerting influence in Tibet.

The signing of this accord clearly implied Tibet's independence in internal affairs; however, the Chinese tried to reassert control in 1910, but could not sustain their claims. When the Qing dynasty fell in 1911, the Dalai Lama drove the Chinese from Lhasa and declared Tibet's total independence to the world.

However, Thubten Gyatso realized just how far behind the rest of the world Tibet really was. In addition to its military lacking modern armaments, Tibet had very few international ties and therefore no global support in times of need.

Historic Tibet was an isolated land, largely due to its position among the Himalayas, which includes Mt. Everest—the highest mountain in the world, peaking at 29,035 feet above sea level. Tibet was challenging to get to in fair weather, and snow blocked mountain passes in winter months, making travel impossible. For many centuries, Lhasa was known as the Forbidden City, and mythology surrounding Tibet touted it as Shangri-La, a utopian world, closed to outsiders. Foreign perceptions of this mythical land were incorrect.

With few outside influences, Tibet was steeped in its own culture. What's more, Tibet was positioned to fall prey to more advanced societies because, as evidenced by its poor showing with a small contingent of British soldiers, Tibetans were unable to protect their own nation. The Thirteenth Dalai Lama began the process of modernizing Tibet, but at the end of his lifetime, reconstruction was far from complete.

In 1932, during his last political statement, he left this prediction:

It may happen that here in the center of Tibet the Religion and the secular administration may be attacked both from the outside and from the inside. Unless we can guard our own country, it will now happen that the Dalai and Panchen Lamas, the Father and the Son ... will be broken down and left without a name. As regards the monasteries and the monks and nuns, their lands and other properties will be destroyed ... The officers of the State, ecclesiastical and secular, will find their lands seized and their other property confiscated, and they themselves made to serve their enemies, or wander about the country as beggars do. All beings will be sunk in great hardship and in overpowering fear; the days and the nights will drag on slowly in suffering.[3]

SIGNS OF THE REBIRTH

Although the Thirteenth Dalai Lama did not speculate when foreign intervention might threaten Tibet again, he seemed to know that it would happen in the impending future and be a heavy burden to his successor. Some Tibetans felt that he designed the time of his death, as bodhisattvas (those who have attained spiritual Nirvana, but choose to return to Earth to help others reach enlightenment) are able to do. He may have decided that his reincarnation—a younger, stronger Dalai Lama—would be better able to handle what the world was about to serve.

On December 17, 1933, one year after his ominous words, the Dalai Lama died at age fifty-eight, after contracting a virus thought to be no more severe than the common cold. Several more years would pass, however, before the validity of his predictions were realized, and the need for a strong leader to continue the Thirteenth Dalai Lama's work was shelved for the time being. Daily life in Tibet would continue, just as it had for thousands of years.

But beforehand, grieving Tibetans prepared for the Dalai Lama's funeral. Unlike preparations made for ordinary people, he would be honored in elaborate services and his body preserved for all to see.

In Tibet, peasants were cremated or sent to the spiritual state between death and reincarnation—called *Bardo*—via sky burial. In this ritual, the family and relatives gather with a monk for farewell, and the body is wrapped in linen bandages and taken to a high cliff. Once there, a hired hand cuts up the body and feeds it to the vultures and crows, as the dead person's last act of generosity.

Dalai Lamas, however, receive higher honors. The Thirteenth Dalai Lama was embalmed, dressed in a gold brocade robe, and seated in the lotus position on a golden throne in the Norbulingka, his winter home in Lhasa. The people who filed past the body to pay homage and lay katas at the departed ruler's feet were comforted by the belief that he would come back to them, as each Dalai Lama had before him.

Usually, a tulku is reborn within one to two years. The present Dalai Lama explained it this way: "Their reincarnations occur whenever conditions are suitable, and do not mean that they leave their state in Nirvana. In simile, it is rather as reflections of the moon may be seen on earth in placid lakes and seas when conditions are suitable, while the moon itself remains in its course in the sky."[4]

Dalai Lamas are tulkus but also bodhisattvas. This refers to their innate desire to return to life, in order to help others attain enlightenment. Bodhisattvas also have the ability to lead those still in the physical world to their tulkus, and certain conditions normally arise within this time to lead Tibetan officials to possible candidates.

Even while the Thirteenth Dalai Lama sat in state, clues leading to his incarnation arose. The first sign was the turning of the Dalai Lama's head, which had been positioned to face south. Without cause, it turned to the northeast overnight. It was repositioned properly, and the next day was found facing eastward again. This was taken as a sign that his reincarnation would be found in the east.

Other signs pointed in this direction, as well. A star-shaped fungus suddenly appeared overnight on the northeastern pillar of the Thirteenth

Dalai Lama's tomb, which was under construction in the Potala, the winter palace of the Dalai Lamas. Unusual cloud formations also appeared in the northeastern sky, in the shapes of elephants, pierced by rainbows. Yet, these signs were not enough to allow the search to commence without further validation.

THE MAGIC OF DALAI LAMAS

Before a search party to find the new Dalai Lama could form, it was necessary for the National Assembly to appoint a regent. These officials were high-ranking monks, traditionally chosen to rule the country until the Dalai Lama reached full maturity and could rule alone. Regents were not the spiritual leaders of the country, nor were they considered to be "living gods," as Buddhists consider Dalai Lamas to be.

Although the Great Thirteenth had expressed the necessity for the regent to be a man with some knowledge of the workings of government and the world outside, Tibetan leaders insisted that the traditional process be followed. They stressed that regents had to be lamas chosen from one of Tibet's three great monasteries—Drepung, Sera, or Ganden—thus ensuring that the new interim head of state would have no administrative experience whatsoever.

The man chosen by lottery was Reting Rinpoché, and in his period of influence (1933–1941), he would help to break down many of the conventions the Great Thirteenth had worked so hard to employ, notably that of not using government resources to further his and other officials' personal businesses.

In his first duty as regent, he ordered a golden mausoleum for the departed Dalai Lama. His second responsibility was to find the Dalai Lama's replacement. He would journey to the sacred lake of Lhamo Lhatso, ninety miles to the southeast of Lhasa, where he hoped for a vision.

Tibet has several holy lakes, although Lhamo Lhatso is its most celebrated. Here, Tibetans believe, the goddess Palden Lhamo promised the first Dalai Lama that she would watch over his successors. Visions from the lake had led to the discovery of the Thirteenth Dalai Lama, nearly sixty years before.

In his book *Portrait of a Dalai Lama,* Sir Charles Bell related the process of divination: "The water of the lake is blue. You watch it from the hillside. A wind arises, and turns the blue water into white. A hole forms in this white water; the hole is blue-black. Clouds form above this hole, and below the clouds, you see images showing future events."[5]

During the vigil, Reting Rinpoché had an elaborate revelation. Floating in the waters, he witnessed the Tibetan alphabet symbols *Ah*, *Ka*, and *Ma*. He also saw a great monastery, with gold and jade rooftops, and from it, a white road leading east to a house with unusual gutters and turquoise tiles. He also saw a brown-and-white dog in the courtyard. He wrote a detailed description of what he saw, and sealed it to keep it confidential.

Next, he consulted the oracle of Samye. In Tibet, magic is a way of life and regarded as one of the natural sciences. In keeping with mystical traditions, oracles exist throughout Tibet and are considered channels of godly information. Tibetan officials consult oracles in all decisions or situations of import, as a matter of state. The oracle of Samye confirmed that Reting Rinpoché had, indeed, seen clues leading to the Fourteenth Dalai Lama. Now they only needed to find him.

After approval from the National Assembly, three search parties, consisting of about forty members each, were sent forth—one to the northeast, one directly east, and one to the southeast. Although officials were convinced that the Tibetan letter *Ah* stood for the Amdo region of Tibet, three parties were sent for two reasons. The most obvious reason was to make a comprehensive search. Another reason was to keep the Chinese off balance, as Chinese warlords still dictated in some portions of eastern Tibet, including Amdo. They worried that if the Chinese learned of their search for the Dalai Lama in Chinese-controlled regions, it would provide another opportunity for China to enter into Tibetan affairs. The Tibetans opted to maintain secrecy and avoid conflict.

For their clandestine pursuit, each search party carried possessions of the Thirteenth Dalai Lama and identical items that had not belonged to him. The oracle of Samye had advised the parties to take two sets of rosaries,[6] one yellow and one black; two small ritual drums, called *damarus*, one plain and one elaborate; and two walking sticks, one bronze-handled and one of iron. In Tibet, it is common for small children to remember people and objects from their past lives, while some can even recite scripture learned in their previous incarnations. The search party intended to present the items to likely candidates for Dalai Lama and, as experience foretold, expected the rightful incarnation to choose from among them those objects belonging to the Great Thirteenth.

A MYSTICAL JOURNEY BEGINS

Setting off in 1936, the party traveling to the northeast was led by Kewtsang Rinpoché, a high lama of Sera monastery. Kewtsang Rinpoché's party traveled for many days, then stopped at a fort—Nakchu Dzong—and spent ten days there gathering supplies. After restocking, they moved on to Sog Tseden Monastery, passed through the Mala Mountains, and then arrived at the home of the Panchen Lama, who is the second most important lama in Tibet.

The Panchen Lama gave the search party the names of three boys who might be potential candidates for Dalai Lama, all of whom lived near Kumbum Monastery, known for its distinctive gold and copper cupolas and roofs trimmed in green jade. The party was convinced that the Tibetan letter *Ka* from Reting Rinpoché's vision referred to Kumbum Monastery.

Once near Kumbum, the searchers were advised by local Tibetan officials to pay homage to the Chinese Muslim warlord and governor, Ma Pu-Feng, in order to continue their search without reprisal. The party members gathered gold, silk, wool, incense, and silver and presented these to the ruler as a token of respect. Although he remained officious and aloof, Ma Pu-Feng granted them formal permission to continue the search after approving their tribute.

When they found the home of the first potential candidate, the party members learned that the boy had died. The second child ran away from them as they approached him, which they deemed to be behavior unlike that of a Dalai Lama. When venturing to visit the third boy in the village of Takster, they discovered themselves at a fork in the hilly path.

A Chinese boy met them and advised them to take the lower road. Along it, they came to Karma Rolpai Dorje, a small village where the Thirteenth Dalai Lama had rested when passing through the area in his trek from Mongolia to Lhasa in October 1906. Monks and villagers had welcomed the Dalai Lama there, and in the crowd was nine-year-old Choekyong Tsering, Lhamo Dhondup's father. Villagers later recalled that the Thirteenth Dalai Lama had looked down over the village of Takster and remarked on its peacefulness and pointed to a house with unusual juniper gutters and a turquoise tile roof, which he thought was particularly attractive. He also left a pair of boots at Karma Rolpai Dorje, as a sign that he would return.

The search party saw the Chinese boy's direction as an omen and thought him, perhaps, a manifestation of a Tibetan deity because when they looked down, they spied a house with turquoise tiles trimming the roof. The gutters were twisted, and a spotted dog was in the courtyard. Although they had discovered a farm resembling Reting Rinpoché's vision, the travelers withheld their enthusiasm and opted for a cautious approach.

In order to interact with the boy informally, Kewtsang Rinpoché donned sheepskins and played the part of servant, while another member of the party, Lobsang Tsewang, acted as leader. They came upon the family clearing snow from their front courtyard during a light storm. Kewtsang Rinpoché told the father that the party had lost their way and asked for shelter for the night. The mother gave them tea, bread, and dried yak meat, and showed Lobsang Tsewang the guest room. The other party members were housed in the kitchen near the stove to keep them warm.

Gyalo Thondup remembered the event. "There seemed to be a lot of servants [with the visitors] and one of them stayed in the kitchen with my mother, helping her stack up logs for the stove, or carrying my little brother, Lhamo Dhondup, around the kitchen in his arms. My little brother seemed to have taken to him."[7]

SIGNS OF A GREAT SPIRIT

As they sat drinking tea with their hosts on the kang, the two-year-old boy crawled up into Kewtsang Rinpoché's lap, stuck his hand inside his robes, and pulled out the lama's rosary beads. He insisted that the rosary was his and asked why Kewtsang Rinpoché wore it. The lama was kind to the child, and told him the rosary was old; he offered to give him a newer one. The boy became angry and continued to demand the rosary. Kewtsang Rinpoché told him he would give it to him if he would tell him his name. "Sera Lama," said the little boy, who seemed to know that the man was from Sera monastery. This surprised Kewtsang Rinpoché, who then asked the name of his "leader," and the boy identified Lobsang Tsewang as well. Not only was this surprising, but the rosary the boy had demanded had been a possession of the Thirteenth Dalai Lama's. Even more astonishing was that the boy addressed the man in the Lhasan dialect, which was virtually unspoken in Amdo.

Early the next morning, the travelers paid the family for their lodging and readied to continue on their way. As they were leaving, the boy tried to go with them and, in tears, pleaded with the men to take him along. He only calmed when the men promised to return.

Three weeks later, they kept their pledge—this time, in order to subject the boy to a battery of tests. On the kang in one bedroom, they set up a low table and placed the objects they had brought from Lhasa on it. First, Kewtsang Rinpoché asked the boy to choose from two identical black rosaries; one was the rosary the child had demanded at his last visit. The boy chose the correct rosary and put it around his neck. He repeated the process with the yellow beads.

Next, he was asked to choose from the walking sticks. At first, the boy put his hand on both sticks, but pulled one hand away and finally chose the correct one. Later, it was learned that both sticks had belonged to the Thirteenth Dalai Lama, but the first had been given to a friend and then to Kewtsang Rinpoché.

Only the drums remained. One was of simple ivory but beautifully crafted. The other was elaborately decorated in brocade, colorful, and potentially more appealing to a child, yet the boy chose the plain drum—the proper choice. With each item chosen, the boy said, "It's mine."[8] The party now thought that proof existed that the *Ah* of Reting Rinpoché's vision did indeed stand for Amdo, the *Ka* for Kumbum, and the *Ma* for Karma Rolpai Dorje. Although this does not seem logical in terms of the Western alphabet, the correlations to the Tibetan alphabet make perfect sense.

Yet there would still have to be a physical inspection of the boy. Eight bodily marks had been found on previous incarnations of the Dalai Lama, and finding them on the boy would be further proof of his identity. Among these are large ears, two small bumps of flesh beneath the shoulder blades, eyebrows that curve up at the ends, marks resembling tiger stripes on the legs, long eyes, and a pattern resembling a seashell on the palm of the hand. The boy had three of these marks.

Sonam Wangdu, a monk in the party, remarked about finding evidence of the new Dalai Lama, "Indeed we were so moved that tears of happiness filled our eyes. Scarcely able to breathe, we could neither sit properly on the mat nor speak a word."[9] The members of the search party were certain they had found "the Great Ocean" of wisdom and compassion. The little boy—Lhamo Dhondup—was the Fourteenth Dalai Lama of Tibet.

To Tibetans, the Dalai Lama is much more than a simple ruler; he is a living Buddha, a god-king, a being considered to have reached enlightenment. They also believe him to be a corporeal manifestation of the bodhisattva of compassion, Chenrezi or Avalokiteshvara, whose head exploded into one thousand fragments when he realized the enormity of his task of working toward the happiness of all sentient beings. It is the vow by which the Dalai Lama lives.

Yet finding him was only the beginning of a long path to his throne. Getting him to Lhasa, where he would be enthroned, would not be easy, and Lhamo Dhondup would have to endure hardship before reaching his true station. Dealing with Ma Pu-Feng again would be the first contest of wills, involving the great treasures of Tibet.

NOTES

1. Colonel Sir Thomas H. Holdich, *Tibet the Mysterious* (New York: Frederick A. Stokes, 1906), p. 329.

2. *Dzong* is the Tibetan word for fort.

3. Quoted in Sir Charles Bell, *Portrait of a Dalai Lama* (London: Wm. Collins, 1946), p. 430.

4. Dalai Lama of Tibet, *My Land and My People* (New York: McGraw, 1962; reprint, New York: Warner Books, 1997), p. 30 (reprint ed.).

5. Quoted in Sir Charles Bell, *Portrait of a Dalai Lama: The Life and Times of the Great Thirteenth* (London: Wisdom Publications, 1987), p. 45 (reprint ed.).

6. Strings of beads on which prayers are counted.

7. Quoted in Mary Craig, *Kundun: A Biography of the Family of the Dalai Lama* (Washington, D.C.: Counterpoint, 1997), p. 15.

8. Tenzin Gyatso, *Freedom in Exile: The Autobiography of the Dalai Lama* (New York: HarperCollins, 1990), p. 12.

9. Quoted in John Avedon, *In Exile from the Land of Snows* (New York: Knopf, 1984; reprint, New York: HarperPerennial, 1997), p. 7 (reprint ed.).

Chapter 3

THE ROAD TO LHASA

Once declared Dalai Lama, Lhamo Dhondup would grow to become the supreme ruler of his country. His subordinates would be, in order of importance, his prime ministers, who controlled the government in his absence or on his behalf; the cabinet, which administered all secular information; the National Assembly, or Tibetan congress; and his chamberlain, a ranking monk official in charge of his staff. This government held control in the central region of Tibet, with Lhasa as its capital.

In the outlying regions of Tibet, leaders of the strongest armies often imposed government. Since the Tibet-China borders were not well defined by Tibet's peasant and nomadic population, these warlords often crossed the borders from China into Tibet, where disorganized nomadic Tibetans were more easily controlled by a superior show of force. Transporting Lhamo Dhondup to Lhasa would be a formidable task, owing to the tyranny of the Chinese Muslim warlord, Ma Pu-Feng, who had come to power in Amdo in 1931.

Ma Pu-Feng proclaimed himself a representative of China, although whether he derived any authority from China was questionable. It is quite possible that he governed Amdo without Chinese affiliation and that he and his followers kept any plunder for themselves.

Kewtsang Rinpoché and the others in the search party were certain that Ma Pu-Feng was bound to make trouble by holding Lhamo Dhondup hostage for ransom—or worse. They deeply feared he would try to use the boy as a pawn to gain favor with China, a country that had tried to control Tibet for centuries. In its more than thousand-year history, China had never been Tibet's master; in the distant past, however, Tibet had dominated China.

ADVENT OF THE YARLUNG KINGS

Organized in familial communities, Tibet's early population swore allegiance to regional tribal chieftains. In this era, village warred against village, and no Tibetan nationalism united them as a country.

Tibet's first king, Nyatri Tsenpo, was proclaimed ruler in the Yarlung Valley, situated in the U-Tsang region of central Tibet, in 127 B.C. Although Tibetan legend held that he came from the sky, in reality, he was an Indian king, named Rupati, who fled over the Himalayas after defeat in the Mahabharata War.[1] Crossing the mighty mountains at that time was an exploit that few men attempted and even fewer survived. Believing that Rupati's advent must, therefore, have been celestial, tribal leaders resolved to make him king. He is the first of the "Yarlung" kings, and forty-one monarchs descended from this first sovereign, to reign for the next thousand years of Tibetan history.

One of the earliest descriptions of Tibetans by outsiders exists in the records of the Tang dynasty, which ruled China during this period: "There are hundreds of thousands of men ready to bear arms, and in order to levy troops they used a golden arrow (as insignia of authority). ...Their armour and helmets are excellent. When they put them on their whole body is covered, with holes just for the eyes. Their bow and their sword never leave them. They prize physical strength and despise old age."[2] Now united, Tibetans became a force of substance, and they were much feared in the Asian world of that time.

The twenty-eighth Yarlung king was the Tibetans' first contact with the teachings of the Lord Buddha. When a volume of Buddha's teachings fell into the king's hands, around 173 B.C., most of the Tibetan populace were practicing Bön—a religion based in animism, or the belief that everything in the universe is alive. Because of fervent Bönpo (people who follow the Bön religion), however, Buddhism did not take hold right away.

Under Songtsen Gampo, the thirty-third Yarlung king (A.D. 609–649), the groundwork was laid for Tibet to become the most powerful country in Asia. His troops conquered territory in Nepal, Bhutan, and Upper Burma, and they invaded China, making parts of western China Tibetan colonies subject to Tibetan taxation of 50,000 rolls of silk per annum.

Songtsen Gampo also sent his minister to study the Sanskrit language and writing in India. Upon the cleric's return to Lhasa, he devised a written Tibetan script, modeled after the Sanskrit alphabet. Through the written word, the king generated a code of behavior by establishing sixteen rules for civil obedience and ten rules applicable to religious services.

The king also introduced Buddhism to the Tibetan court. Although most people in modern Tibet were monogamous, the taking of multiple marriage partners by both men and women was tolerated, and King Songtsen Gampo had multiple wives. When he married both a Chinese princess and the daughter of the king of Nepal, he did so to solidify relations with nations bordering Tibet in the east and west. Both women were ardently Buddhist. As part of her dowry, the Chinese princess brought a huge golden statue of the Buddha, and Songtsen Gampo built Tibet's first temple—Jokhang—to house it. The king was converted, and Buddhism began to take on an important role in Tibetan life as it spread through his court. He is known as the First Religious King.

In 754, Trisong Detsen, the thirty-seventh Yarlung king, took the throne and brought Tibet to the height of empire. Known as the Second Religious King, Trisong Detsen promoted the spread of Buddhism by employing 108 Indian scholars to translate the Buddhist scriptures from Sanskrit to Tibetan. He also had Tibet's first monastery built—Samye—around 779. During his reign, the first seven Tibetan monks were trained, which would lead to the overwhelming adoption of Tibetan life based in religion. He encouraged his people to throw down their weapons and take up the philosophies of Buddhism, which afford respect to all living things, regardless of stature. To the Buddhist, a bug's life is as important as any man's. Trisong Detsen promoted peace, although his philosophy was not universally accepted at that time.

The move toward greater serenity continued into the reign of the Third Religious King, Ralpachen, when diplomatic relations with China were established. A pillar outside the Jokhang temple, erected between 821 and 822, speaks of the two countries as independent nations:

> Tibet and China shall abide by the frontiers of which they are now in occupation. All to the east is the country of great China; and all to the west is, without question, the country of great Tibet. Henceforth, on neither side shall there be waging of war nor seizing of territory. . . . This solemn agreement has established a great epoch when Tibetans shall be happy in the land of Tibet, and Chinese in the land of China.[3]

Ralpachen also issued a decree stating that seven households should support each monk. Many more temples were constructed, and more Indian Buddhist masters were invited to Tibet to further Tibetan religious training.

However, the golden period of the three great religious kings soon ended. In 838, Ralpachen was assassinated, and his brother, who was brutally opposed to Buddhism, became the forty-second and last of the Yarlung kings. He destroyed the institutions set up by his predecessors, forced monks from monasteries, and threw the country into a state of distress. For more than three hundred years, Tibet was reduced to a hodgepodge of feuding factions.

A HISTORY OF PATRONAGE

Buddhism did not regain its hold over the Tibetan population until the eleventh century, when it was reintroduced by the Indian scholar Atisha, who came to Tibet in 1042. He authored *A Lamp on the Path to Enlightenment,* which revived the Buddhist doctrine and dispelled many of the misconceptions about the belief system that were common at the time.

By the twelfth century, Buddhism had supplanted Bön as the national religion, yet Buddhism was the only common factor among the warring factions of a fragmented Tibetan society. Reunification of the country came at the price of independence when, in 1207, Tibetan tribal leaders decided to offer tribute to the Mongolian warlord and founder of the Mongol Empire, Genghis Khan, then at the edge of Tibetan borders, poised to overrun them. A simple agreement, whereby Tibet paid annual taxes to Mongolia, restrained them from further military action for thirty-two years. Then, in 1239, Tibet failed to pay. This default spurred the grandson of Genghis Khan, Godan Khan, to invade the territory, burn Reting monastery, and slaughter five hundred Tibetans.

However, upon ravaging the country and declaring supremacy, the Mongols did not assume control of Tibet. They assessed the country's taxation potential and organized Tibet into districts. They had no desire to destroy Tibetan culture or religion, only to learn from it.

Also a Buddhist, Godan Khan desired religious training from Sakya Pandit, the leader of the Sakya, or White, sect. (At that time, Sakya was one of the three sects of Mahayana Buddhism, the school of Buddhism to which Tibetan Buddhism belongs. The other two were the Nyingma, or the Old School, sect, and the Kagyü, the school of oral tradition or the Red sect.) When Sakya Pandit agreed to help the khan, he received spiritual authority over all of central Tibet. Thus began the priest-patron relationship of Tibet with other nations. Through their Mongol alliance, Tibet became loosely associated with China when in 1279, Kublai Khan finally suppressed the Sung dynasty completely and made it part of his Yuan dynasty. Still, there was no demand for Tibet to become part of a unified Mongol empire, and Tibet was left alone to run its internal affairs.

In 1368, the priest-patron bond between Mongolia and Tibet was broken when Chinese nationalists drove the last Mongol emperor from China. Although Tibet was again without a military protector, its government made no overtures to the new Chinese rulers to continue a similar relationship. Tibet maintained independence for the next three hundred years.

THE PATH TO DALAI LAMA

During this time of autonomy, much in-fighting occurred between rival monasteries. Other sects had noticed the eminence of the Sakyas rise under Mongol influence. Now the other factions, along with the Sakyas, realized an opportunity for one ruler to seize eminence. Yet none emerged until after 1357, when the great lama and leader Tsonkapa was born.

He came to central Tibet from Amdo in 1372 and was appalled by the decline in morals in the religious community, especially in the realm of celibacy, a supposed monastic ideal. He began to preach reform, emphasizing strict monastic vows and diligent study as the path to Buddhahood. His charismatic appeal attracted many followers and ultimately helped him to found Ganden monastery in 1409.

His followers became a new sect—the Gelugpas, also known as the Yellow Sect or the Virtuous Ones. They discarded the previous years' animosities and violence among rival monks, and condemned sexual indiscretions. They returned to the true Buddhist spiritual path, based in strict morality.

After the death of Tsonkapa in 1417, his position at the head of the Gelugpa sect was filled by one of his disciples, Gedun Drub. The new ruler was instrumental in extending the influence of the Gelugpas southward, as he founded the famous monastery of Tashilhunpho—the future home of the Panchen Lamas—near the town of Shigatse in 1445. During his time, other great monasteries of Tibet were also founded by followers of Tsonkapa, including the monasteries of Ganden, Drepung, and Sera. When Gedun Drub died in 1474, his supporters recognized him as having achieved Buddhahood, after a long and noble life.

In 1475, a child was born who later remembered certain elements of a past life. He was able to recognize things he had never seen before, and he clearly seemed to the high lamas to be the reincarnation of Gedun Drub. When the boy was declared Gedun Drub's descendant, the tulku system of choosing successors came into effect. Although originally developed by the Kargyu sect, the Gelugpa sect's system of tulku lineage came to the forefront and, with continued Mongol influence, helped the Gelugpas rule Tibet into the twentieth century. Not only did the system prevent future dissension among the sects, but it also allowed boys to be trained in spiritual control from a young age. The new High Lama of Drepung was renamed Gedun Gyatso. In Tibetan, *Gyatso* means "ocean," and the name has passed to each Dalai Lama since that time.

But it was not until the third incarnation—in Sonam Gyatso—that the title Dalai Lama was born. He converted Altan Khan, leader of the Tumed Mongol tribe and a descendant of Kublai Khan, to Buddhism in 1578 and reformed the Mongol alliance. The Mongols were desirable partners on two fronts: they would keep outsiders from invading Tibet, and keep the Gelugpas in control. The Mongols benefited through cultural advancement from their Bön roots to Buddhism, which emanated a higher form of spiritualism and raised them from barbarism to a common ground with the refined Chinese.

To seal the bond, Altan Khan and Sonam Gyatso swore friendship and bestowed titles on each other at the Mongol court. Altan Khan was dubbed "King of the Turning Wheel of Wisdom," while Sonam Gyatso received the title Dalai, which in Mongolian means "ocean," alluding to his ocean of wisdom. Therefore, with Sonam Gyatso, who was already a lama, or teacher, the term *Dalai Lama* came to be. He accepted the title for himself and, posthumously, for the two spiritual rulers who came before him— Gedun Drub and Gedun Gyatso—making him the third Dalai Lama.

The title Dalai Lama was mainly spiritual until 1642, when the Mongol leader Gushri Khan made the Fifth Dalai Lama, Ngwang Lobsang Gyatso, both spiritual and political leader of the country. To strengthen his new position, the "Great Fifth," as he is still known today, visited China. The Manchu emperor, who later established the Qing dynasty and ruled China until 1911, received him as a leader and an equal, and the position of Dalai Lama has maintained an air of sanctity and authority ever since.

THE MISERY OF KUMBUM

Three centuries later, when Ma Pu-Feng learned that a potential Dalai Lama had been found in his domain, the search party feared there would be trouble. To avoid conflict, they brought several local boys between two and three years old to Ma Pu-Feng's headquarters in Xining to be tested. None of the children could choose more than two or three of the Thirteenth Dalai Lama's possessions from the dual sets brought forth by the search party. The party hoped this would be sufficient evidence for the governor that the next Dalai Lama would not be from his district.

Ma Pu-Feng, however, was not so easily dissuaded. Informers had given him leads to Lhamo Dhondup, so he ordered the boy and a few others to appear before him in a private audience. In his own test, Ma Pu-Feng offered each boy a box of sweets. Some took several. Some were too ashamed to taste even one. Lhamo Dhondup, however, took just one sweet from the box, and returned to his seat to eat it in silence. His manner and restraint assured Ma Pu-Feng that Lhamo Dhondup was the tulku of the Dalai Lama before.

When the search party requested to take the boy to Lhasa for further testing, Ma Pu-Feng denied them. He insisted that he be paid 100,000 Chinese dollars as ransom for the boy, an enormous sum for that time. Feeling they had no choice but to pay the demand, the Tibetan delegation sent word to Lhasa and had the money delivered.

Yet Ma Pu-Feng was not so easily appeased. When he saw how readily his demand had been met, he demanded another 100,000 Chinese dollars for the military government; 100,000 for his staff, to keep them from carrying tales to the Chinese government; 100,000 for Kumbum Monastery; 20,000 for the escort he planned to send to Lhasa with the boy; and 10,000 for the time and cost of arranging the new Dalai Lama's departure—an additional 330,000 Chinese dollars. He also demanded that a full set of the Thirteenth Dalai Lama's clothing and a full set of the Lord Buddha's teachings, written in gold, be delivered to Kumbum Monastery before he would agree to the boy's release.

The Tibetans were outraged at Ma Pu-Feng's conditions, and had already met with difficulty in obtaining the funds to satisfy his first demand. They told Ma Pu-Feng that his request was unreasonable, that the boy was not the declared Dalai Lama, and that other choices had to be examined. Ma Pu-Feng rejected their pleas, and insisted that the boy be housed at Kumbum monastery while they raised the necessary payments.

When he entered Kumbum, Lhamo Dhondup's childhood virtually ended. He later wrote, "There now began a somewhat unhappy period of my life. My parents did not stay long and soon I was alone amongst these new and unfamiliar surroundings."[4]

The new Dalai Lama did have two family members at the monastery—brothers Thubten Jigme Norbu, now Takster Rinpoché, and five-year-old Lobsang Samten, who had been sent to Kumbum for studies when he was three years old. Now, Takster Rinpoché had two homesick siblings to watch over. He said of Lhamo Dhondup, "Dissolved in tears he begged us to take him home. Lobsang Samten was the first to join little Lhamo Dhondup in his sobs, but long before I too dissolved into tears."[5]

The Dalai Lama remembers waiting all day for Lobsang Samten to come out from his study room so that the two could play together. He also remembers Lobsang Samten's teacher, who held him inside his robe and comforted him with an offering of a ripe peach.

However, bitter memories involved the boys' uncle, who became enraged over Lhamo Dhondup's scattering and mixing up of his loose-leaf scriptures. The uncle slapped Lhamo Dhondup hard; however, it was not an isolated event. As their uncle was unused to the activities of two small boys, he corrected his nephews often and harshly. The boys would run away and hide in the huge monastery for hours, presumably to punish their uncle for his cruel behavior toward them. They delighted in the fact that when they were found and the fury over losing the intended Dalai Lama had passed, their uncle softened considerably and pled for their forgiveness, offering candies to his young nephews as restitution.

A GREAT JOURNEY

About eighteen months after Lhamo Dhondup's arrival at Kumbum, the delegation from Lhasa finally organized Ma Pu-Feng's ransom via transient Muslim traders. The traders agreed to lend the amount Ma Pu-Feng required in exchange for the same amount in Indian rupees once they reached Lhasa. This deal was to the merchants' benefit. Due to a higher exchange rate, they would receive more rupees for the Chinese dollars. On the Tibetan side, since Ma Pu-Feng was also Muslim and there was an implied kinship between him and the merchants, the traders guaranteed to see to Ma Pu-Feng's satisfaction, eliminating the possibility of further extortion. The British, who ruled India at the time, also helped seal the bargain by agreeing to a duty-free transport of the rupees into Tibet, thus assuring the Dalai Lama's release.

Ma Pu-Feng then agreed to allow the boy and his party to go on to Lhasa, on the condition that a member of the Lhasan party be left behind until the clothing of the Thirteenth Dalai Lama and the golden scriptures were delivered to Kumbum monastery. The hostage, however, soon escaped Ma Pu-Feng's custody and returned to Lhasa on his own.

Within three weeks of the departure agreement, a traveling party was assembled to accompany the new Dalai Lama to Lhasa. Takster Rinpoché was left behind, as was Lhamo Dhondup's sister, Tsering Dolma, who was pregnant with her first child. The party did, however, include Lhamo

Dhondup's parents, six-year-old Lobsang Samten, and eleven-year-old Gyalo Thondup, along with the search party and the Muslims, who went along to assure the loan. The company comprised 50 travelers and 350 horses and mules. They set off on July 21, 1939, just two weeks after Lhamo Dhondup's fourth birthday.

The departure was bittersweet for the parents of the golden child. Although they were almost certain Lhamo Dhondup would be named Dalai Lama, the members of the search party would only tell them that he was in the running. Even filled with hope, leaving all they had known in their lifetimes, in addition to their two older children, was heart-wrenching for them. Diki Tsering wrote: "Our relatives wept that they might never see us again. We Amdo folk are very emotional and sentimental. . . . Our relatives journeyed with us for several days, and then they returned to their homes. I wept so much that I was blinded most of the day of our departure."[6]

Most of the party rode on horses and mules, while Diki Tsering traveled in her own palanquin of green cotton with small lattice windows. Lobsang Samten and Lhamo Dhondup rode together in a yellow brocade carriage hung on two poles (called a treljam), carried on the backs of mules. When the terrain became rough, the treljam would have to be carried by the monks of the search party with considerable strain. Lobsang Samten remembered, "Lhamo Dhondup and I played, teased each other and fought to the brink of tears in the palanquin."[7] Often the treljam would sway from side to side during these tussles, and the boys' mother was called to chastise them. Although Lobsang Samten was older and bigger than his brother, the smaller boy usually won their battles. The Dalai Lama wrote, "Lobsang Samten was so good-natured that he could not bring himself to use his superior strength against me."[8]

Every day, the troupe plodded along for about ten miles from dawn until noon, at which time they would set up their yak tents for the night. Aside from a few nomads, who came to ask for the Dalai Lama's blessing, the party saw very few people during their journey. At Nagchuka, however, a cavalry detachment of the Tibetan army delighted the children with a display of trick riding. Although he had not been officially confirmed as Dalai Lama, Lhamo Dhondup's people, having heard the rumors, afforded him the respect and deference due his impending station.

THE NEW OCEAN OF WISDOM

When Lhamo Dhondup was safely away from Chinese control, the National Assembly was summoned to confirm him as the Fourteenth Dalai

Lama, which they did in a unanimous decision. Immediately following, a retinue of senior officials was sent from Lhasa to greet him.

After having spent three months on the road, the travelers met this first welcoming party at the Thutopchu River, and the caravan grew. The welcoming party brought along supplies for the travelers and four yak-skin boats, to take the contingent and their supplies across the river.

A few days later, another party from Lhasa welcomed them, including the Nechung oracle; a Geshe, or doctor of Metaphysics from Drepung Monastery; and a minister from the cabinet. The minister laid katas at Lhamo Dhondup's feet and prostrated himself three times in the Mendel Tensum—a triple offering of reverence and homage, in which he pledged his speech, body, and mind to the boy. At this moment, his parents were finally assured that their son was, indeed, the Fourteenth Dalai Lama.

To solidify the claim, the party also brought along a declaration from the regent, the cabinet, and the National Assembly, proclaiming Lhamo Dhondup as Dalai Lama. On his parents were bestowed the titles Gyayum, meaning "great mother," and Gyayap, meaning "great father" and they were offered new clothes. Although his father donned the re-splendent clothing of a cabinet minister, his mother preferred to continue wearing traditional garb. As she related, "Government officials ... pre-sented me with pearl and coral patus, the Lhasa women's headdresses, and brocade dresses and other accessories worn by the women of Lhasa. I re-fused to wear the patu. I said that I . . . would not feel comfortable with the patu, which was too heavy."[9]

Much changed quickly, whether the family of Choekyong Tsering was ready for the transformation in their lives or not. Lhamo Dhondup would no longer be called by his birth name but Kundun, meaning "presence of the Buddha," even by his own family. The boy was dressed in yellow bro-cade robes and a yellow, peaked fur hat and transferred to his own golden palanquin. At that point, the procession became majestic. Monks carried tall banners before him and one held a huge iridescent umbrella of pea-cock feathers over his transport. Deep trumpets sounded. A cloud of dust mingled with the smoke of incense, as monks and lamas met their new Dalai Lama in every town and village.

On October 6, 1939, at Rigya on the Doguthang Plain, two miles east of Lhasa, the procession stopped. The four-year-old boy was then taken into the Great Peacock—a tent of bright yellow, a color used only for Dalai Lamas. Previously owned by the Thirteenth Dalai Lama, the tent was roofed by a blue and white canopy, decorated with blue designs out-side and embroidered patterns of blue, red, and yellow spirals inside.

Golden figures on the roof pole included peacocks, providing the tent with its name.

Sitting on a carved wooden throne, specifically used for welcoming new infant Dalai Lamas, the child held a yellow tassel in his right hand. With it, he blessed leading monastic officials who passed before him. Soon, representatives from neighboring countries, including Britain, Bhutan, Nepal, and China, joined the procession, while the small boy sat—unsmiling, reserved, and dignified. His patience and self-possession impressed everyone in attendance. He seemed suited to his new station in life, as if he had been born to it. He wrote of that day: "I felt as if I were in a dream. I felt as if I were in a great park covered with beautiful flowers, while soft breezes blew across it and peacocks elegantly danced before me."[10]

When the parade continued into the city of Lhasa on October 8, sixteen nobles, dressed in round, red-tasseled hats and green satin robes, carried the new Dalai Lama in his golden palanquin. Cabinet members, astrologers, Reting Rinpoché, the prime minister, the Dalai Lama's family, and many other ranking monks and officials joined in amid music from horns, cymbals, drums, and gongs. Thousands of peasants, with heads solemnly bowed in reverence, lined the route, dressed in their fine chubas and every piece of jewelry they owned. Every window was shut, as no one should look at the Dalai Lama from above. Into the mix came the sounds of "God Save the King," played by the Tibetan army band, which had learned the tune from British military instructors during the reign of Thubten Gyatso.

The Nechung oracle met the party as well, wearing a headdress of white feather plumes and a golden crown. He carried a sword and a bow, and had a polished silver mirror across his chest. As is true of all Tibetan oracles, he was soon possessed by his protective deity and began to hiss, puff his cheeks, roll his eyes, and extend his legs from side to side in the ritual dance. Although he rushed at the palanquin and stuck his head quickly inside as a show of reverence, the child went unphased and offered his hand in blessing. The oracle offered the boy a kata, which the new Dalai Lama accepted and then placed around the oracle's neck.

More well-wishers were on the scene in Lhasa, and upon the new Dalai Lama's arrival, he was taken to Norbulingka, the summer palace of the Dalai Lama. This would be his home until his final enthronement at the Potala—the one-thousand-room palace of the Dalai Lama, where they would place him on the Lion Throne.

The new Dalai Lama would spend his last days of a carefree existence at Norbulingka. At four years old, he would soon assume the spiritual leadership of the people of Tibet.

NOTES

1. A great epic poem, *The Mahabharata* (akin to Homer's *Iliad*), was written in Sanskrit around 400 B.C. to relay details of the Mahabharata War between the Pandava and Kaurava families in northern India, purportedly during Rupati's time.

2. Quoted in David Snellgrove and Hugh Richardson, *A Cultural History of Tibet* (New York: Praeger, 1968), p. 29.

3. Quoted in Hugh E. Richardson, *Tibet and Its History* (London: Oxford University Press, 1962), app. I, pp. 244–245.

4. Tenzin Gyatso, *Freedom in Exile*, p. 12.

5. Quoted in Mary Craig, *Kundun*, p. 60.

6. Diki Tsering, *Dalai Lama, My Son*, pp. 97–98.

7. Quoted in Mary Craig, *Kundun*, p. 64.

8. Tenzin Gyatso, *Freedom in Exile*, p. 14.

9. Diki Tsering, *Dalai Lama, My Son*, p. 104.

10. The Dalai Lama of Tibet, *My Land and My People*, p. 17.

Chapter 4

ASSUMING THE LIFE
OF A MONK

His Holiness arrived at one of his new homes, the Norbulingka, on October 8, 1939. Although the Norbulingka was the traditional summer palace of the Dalai Lama, he would remain there until his formal installation, when he would move to the Potala, the winter home of the Dalai Lama and seat of the Tibetan government. As the investiture would not occur until shortly after the Tibetan New Year, which occurs around the full moon each February, the Dalai Lama was able to frolic and enjoy being a boy just a little longer, although his new life was far removed from the life he knew in his humble home in Takster.

Just two miles outside Lhasa, the Norbulingka began construction under the auspices of the Seventh Dalai Lama, Kelsang Gyatso (1708–1757). The Dalai Lama prized the wooded area, and each summer, he bathed in its mineral springs. In 1755, he erected a palace nearby, the Kelsang Palace, and fulfilled his office from there each summer, as did all Dalai Lamas to follow.

The Eighth Dalai Lama, Jampel Gyatso (1758–1804), was responsible for significantly expanding the Norbulingka's area by adding three temples and perimeter walls around the southeast section. The park-like atmosphere took shape then with the planting of blossoming gardens and arbors, which included both fruit trees and evergreens brought to Lhasa from all parts of Tibet. A host of gardeners was needed to keep the grounds and the paths within the Norbulingka in order.

Major additions to the Norbulingka took place under the Thirteenth Dalai Lama, who also improved the gardens. In 1930, he had the Chensel Lingka area in the northwest built, which included three additional

palaces. However, palaces in all parts of the park were little more than ornately decorated houses.

At the time of Lhamo Dhondup, the general name Norbulingka included the Norbulingka and the Chensel Lingka. The eastern half included three sections: the palace, the opera, and government offices. The
palace section held two palaces, and the opera grounds included an open-
air stage and gardens, where the Opera Festival was celebrated each year.
A courtyard for practicing the Tibetan art of debate and a bathhouse were
also in this part of the park. Lush gardens surrounded both structures.

The Norbulingka's most dramatic area, the Lake Palace, filled the
southwest area. In its center lake, three islands were connected to each
other and to the land by short bridges. A palace stood on each island. A
horse pavilion and a row of buildings, which housed valuable gifts from
Chinese emperors and other foreign nations, were just south of the lake.

The western portion of the park included three sections—the palace
section, the forest, and the fields. In the northern sector were compounds
for cattle and sheep, and the fields held a platform used by the Nechung
oracle during divinations. Horse races and kite flying also took place in
the fields.

Surrounding the entire Norbulingka were two sets of walls. The inner
wall marked the space where only the Dalai Lama and his attendants were
permitted. Between the inner "yellow" wall and the outer wall, officials
and the Dalai Lama's "royal family" lived.

Only visitors wearing Tibetan dress were allowed to enter the Norbulingka, and bodyguards were posted at the gates to make sure no Western
hats, which were very popular in Tibet during Lhamo Dhondup's time,
nor shoes made their way into the park. Nobles of high rank received a
presentation of arms from the guards, while lower-ranking Tibetans received only a salute.

Outside the yellow wall, the gates were heavily protected, and only the
Dalai Lama and his guardians could pass. Intermittently, dog kennels were
built into the wall, and savage Tibetan mastiff guard dogs patrolled the
perimeter, as far as their yak-hair leashes would allow.

SETTLING INTO A NEW HOME

The Dalai Lama arrived at the Norbulingka when the trees and flowers
were in bloom, which delighted him. Yet before the family was even settled,
his mother was astonished by his actions. "I was surprised to see His Holiness breaking the seals of the many trunks he found in his quarters.... Finally he found what he was looking for, a small box covered in brocade.

I asked him what he was doing, and he told me that inside this box was a tooth. When he opened it, indeed there was a tooth, which had belonged to the thirteenth Dalai Lama."[1]

Shortly thereafter, the travelers were treated to a welcoming ceremony with tea and pastry. Afterward, the family of Lhamo Dhondup was directed to separate quarters in a farmhouse known as Gyatso, outside the yellow wall.

At Gyatso, the Dalai Lama's parents were surprised to find gifts of tea, butter, silk, rice, carpets, flour, and brocades. They were also supplied with a staff, including interpreters, stablemen, water bearers, maids, secretaries, and cooks.

Three monks became the Dalai Lama's attendants through appointment. The Master of the Ritual, the Master of the Kitchen, and the Master of the Robes were all monks. The Dalai Lama formed an intense bond with the Master of the Kitchen and for a time would not let the man out of his sight. Even seeing the hem of his robe behind a closed door was enough comfort for the young Dalai Lama, who felt serene knowing that the Master of the Kitchen was nearby.

The boy also loved the summer gardens and was fond of running and boating. The gardens—filled with poplar, willow, juniper, apple, pear, peach, walnut, and apricot trees—were a superb place to play and to pick and savor the delicious fruit from the trees. The main lake was full of carp. Lobsang Samten often accompanied the Dalai Lama outdoors, and the boys sometimes fished in the pond with a net, but they always released any fish they caught. The boys thought of the fish as pets, which were so tame that they often rose to the surface at the sound of a rower's oar, asking to be fed.

ASSUMING THE TEMPORAL THRONE

This pastoral lifestyle continued for four months, until the Dalai Lama's official installation on February 22, 1940. The regent, who had conferred with the National Assembly and the state astrologers, fixed the date as potentially auspicious. Preparations were made, and dignitaries from foreign governments were invited.

On investiture day, the Dalai Lama was taken to the Potala Palace, the largest structure in Tibet. Begun in the seventh century by King Songtsen Gampo, the Potala served various functions, most prominently as the winter home of the Dalai Lama and the seat of Tibetan government. The Potala leans against and caps an area known as Red Hill, and during war times, it served as a fort. Within its enormous 130,000 square meters of interior space sit tombs of eight previous Dalai Lamas, palaces, chapels, courtyards, assembly halls, towers, and exquisite works of art from Tibet and around the world.

The most important structures within the Potala are the White Palace and the Red Palace. The White Palace houses dormitories, a Buddhist seminary, offices, a printing house, and the Dalai Lama's living quarters. Three parallel sets of vertical stairs lead to the inside, with the middle stairway reserved for use by only the Dalai Lama. Huge murals line the entrance, showing scenes of the construction of the Potala and Jokhang Temple.

In the Red Palace, the Great West Hall holds murals describing the Great Fifth Dalai Lama's life, and is adorned with finely carved columns. The Red Palace also holds three chapels, one of which holds the three golden dome-shaped monuments of the Fifth, Tenth, and Twelfth Dalai Lamas, where their mummified and perfumed bodies lie. West of the Great West Hall stands the monument of the Great Thirteenth, which is coated with nearly one ton of gold foil. Before it lays a sacred, symbolic painting—a mandala—made from more than 200,000 pearls and other gems.

The origin of the Potala's name is uncertain; however, when translating Buddhist script from Indian to Tibetan, Songtsen Gampo's minister wrote of Riwo Potala, in India—the mystical abode of the god of compassion. As Dalai Lamas are thought to be the embodiment of the god, it would make sense for this to be the source of its name. The familiar name of the Potala is the Palace of 1,000 Rooms.

The Dalai Lama's initiation ceremony was held in the Hall of All Good Deeds of the Spiritual and Temporal Worlds, located in the eastern portion of the palace. Hours before he was to make his entrance, officials laid out the royal gifts. Among them were a brick of gold from the Calcutta Mint, two horses, ten bags of silver, three rifles, a gold watch and chain, field glasses, a picnic basket, six rolls of broadcloth, and a six-foot elephant tusk.

The procession into the hall began with servants, wearing green tunics and red-tasseled hats and carrying the Dalai Lama's food and clothes. Attendants carried tall banners, hoping to ward off evil spirits. Chinese officials, high lamas, and the state oracle all followed, as did the head monks of the Potala, wearing red robes. Various uniformed men followed behind them. These men were the standard bearers and the carriers of the Dalai Lama's palanquin. Behind him came the regent, in golden silk, riding an ornately decorated horse, led by two grooms. Then came the Dalai Lama's family and various lamas and monks from the surrounding monasteries.

Long resonant chants combined with the roar of the four-yard-long "great horn." Hand bells tinkled, and silver trumpets cried out. Drums of all types sounded, from the tiny handheld damaru to deep base drums.

Immediately upon his arrival, the boy was lifted onto his Lion Throne—the seat of the Dalai Lama—which was built in accordance with Tibetan scripture. Carved in wood, the square throne is gilded, encrusted in jewels, and supported by eight carved and gilded snow lions— the Tibetan national symbol. Because no one may sit higher than the Dalai Lama, the throne is between six and seven feet tall and padded with five cushions, each covered in brocade of a different color. Owing to the chill in the February day, the new Dalai Lama was wrapped in blankets. A table before the throne held his seals of office.

To open the ceremony, the regent presented the Mendel Tensum prostrations and three symbolic offerings—a golden figure of the Buddha of Eternal Life, representing wishes for a long life; a book of scripture regarding the Buddha, representing the Dalai Lama's duty to propagate and elucidate Buddhism; and a miniature multitiered container holding a holy relic, representing a wish for him to have thoughts like those of the Buddha's. Various officials then offered katas to the new ruler, who blessed the monks by touching his forehead to theirs, and blessed the prime minister—a layman—by touching the man's head with both hands.

The Dalai Lama was then presented with a sweet-tasting herb in a small golden cup and saucer as a symbol of good luck. This herb is presented during all Tibetan ceremonies. Tea and sweetened rice were then offered to all in attendance. Meanwhile, monks engaged in debate, and performances by mimes and musicians amused the audience. Afterward, fruit and a Tibetan cake were offered as dessert.

In the next part of the ceremony, the regent again presented the Mendel Tensum to the Dalai Lama on behalf of the Tibetan government. The Golden Wheel and the White Conch, symbols of spiritual and temporal power, were then presented to His Holiness. Afterward, each official and guest presented the Mendel Tensum before the Lion Throne and offered good wishes and gifts to the new ruler. The process lasted for more than five hours. Even so, the young Dalai Lama never fidgeted or stopped paying attention.

When the blessings ended, the Dalai Lama received his seals of office and in his first official act, fixed seals upon documents bearing orders for the monasteries. At four and a half, the extraordinary boy seemed happy and secure in his royal future.

Shortly after the installation ceremony, the Dalai Lama and his brother Lobsang Samten were taken to Jokhang Temple and initiated as monks.

Llamo Dhondup's head was shaved, and his name changed by the regent. Lhamo Dhondup would now be Jamphel Ngawang Lobsang Yeshe Tenzin Gyatso, meaning "holy one, tender glory, mighty in speech, compassionate one, learned defender of the faith, ocean of wisdom." His official signature would be Tenzin Gyatso, the Fourteenth Dalai Lama.

DIFFICULT ADJUSTMENTS

Although the Dalai Lama's family was to live in a newly constructed residence, the boy was required to live in the Potala. Such a huge palace was very imposing for the small boy, and it was difficult for him to adjust, since it was more like a museum than a home. The Potala was cold in winter and had an unbearable smell in the summer from the underlying sewers. It was dark and filled with monks, all of whom were much older than the Potala's newest resident.

He was provided the Great Fifth's bedroom on the top floor of the palace, which was its seventh story. He remembered, "Everything in it was ancient and decrepit and behind the drapes that hung across each of the four walls lay deposits of centuries-old dust."[2] He also wrote of the altar, which stood at one end of the room, where butter lamps (bowls of rancid butter into which a wick is set) and dishes of food were placed in offering to the Buddha each day. The food attracted mice, which ran atop the curtains of his bed at night, dripping urine onto his blankets below.

His family was ill at ease in many respects as well. Most disconcerting was that they did not speak the Lhasan dialect. The Tibetan language differed so widely that there was little comparison between one region's vernacular and another's. Takster Rinpoché wrote:

> Lobsang Samten was only two years older than the Dalai Lama, and their interests were therefore quite similar. They already talked to each other exclusively in Lhasa dialect, whereas all the other members of the family spoke to each other in the Amdo dialect, and were only gradually accustoming themselves to High Tibetan. However, in the presence of the Dalai Lama we all did our best to speak it in the polite Lhasa fashion, making as few mistakes as possible.[3]

As country people of Amdo, Diki Tsering and Choekyong Tsering were not used to their new roles as aristocrats. Diki Tsering continued to wear the homespun clothing from her own region and never saw the need to pose as a high lady of Lhasa. For this, the women of the nobility criticized her. She had only one good friend—Madame Lalu, who helped her deal with the upper class.

Choekyong Tsering, on the other hand, allowed his new status to change him. As the head of the family, he was given to the position of kung, akin to the rank of a royal duke. Diki Tsering often reprimanded her husband for shouting at the servants, and almost from the beginning, he demanded high sums in cash from the Dalai Lama's cabinet.

In June 1940, the cabinet offered Choekyong Tsering two estates from which to choose suitable living accommodations. He accepted them both and asked for more. Although Diki Tsering was much loved by everyone that came to know her, in the cabinet's eyes, the Dalai Lama's parents were a unit. A Tibetan official once wrote: "The Dalai Lama's parents again complained that they [could] not maintain and support themselves with the two estates and they demanded three more estates."[4]

For both parents, life was entirely different than it had ever been. They had no backbreaking work and no animals to tend, although Choekyong Tsering still kept a stable of horses, and Gyalo Thondup had been sent to school in Taiwan. Yet Diki Tsering did not enjoy a life of idleness. She arose at dawn, performed two hundred prostrations, and then said her prayers. She spent most of her time in the gardens at her estate and went to sleep at nine.

The Dalai Lama was finding it hard to adjust to his new life in the Potala as well. During the day, while Lobsang Samten was in classes studying, the Dalai Lama, still too young for formal schooling, roamed the huge Potala, exploring its incredible storerooms. He especially loved those that held suits of armor, weapons, and any kind of mechanical device. He amused himself with music boxes and mechanical toys, but they would soon be in pieces, as he was consumed with curiosity about how things worked and so took them apart. Some of these gifts had come from the czars of Russia, and the Dalai Lama's attendants cringed as the valuable antiques were dissembled. Yet they were soon amazed at the facility with which the child put the priceless treasures back together.

He was not always successful, however. Once, when reassembling an old clock, the mechanism ran far beyond its normal speed. The teeth of the musical comb shattered and flew off in every direction. The Dalai Lama closed his eyes and ducked for the ten seconds the clock sent its shrapnel forth, and was lucky not to have been blinded.

His was a lonely existence. He made friends with the older monks and with the sweepers, or room attendants. Many of them were ill-educated men who had come from a tour of duty in the Tibetan army. Their task was to keep the rooms of the Potala tidy, and to see that the floors were always polished. As he enjoyed sliding on the floors, the Dalai Lama was adamant about that particular task's satisfactory completion.

At the end of the day, the Dalai Lama often waited outside his brother's classroom. Though they still fought heartily, the two were dependent on one another for companionship, as they were the only children in the palace. Yet the day drew near for the Dalai Lama's own educational responsibilities—a time when he would train his mind to the disciplines of his future duties.

A STUDENT OF ANCIENT SCRIPTURE

The Dalai Lama's formal education began at six years of age, and was overseen by his first, second, and third tutors. The regent, Reting Rinpoché, who had seen the vision in the sacred lake and who had formally installed the Dalai Lama as the Tibetan leader, was his senior tutor. Tathag Rinpoché, a spiritual and kind lama, was appointed his junior tutor. Once lessons were through, he and the boy would often engage in casual talks and joking, helping the boy to feel a measure of kinship, which he so badly desired. The third tutor was Kewtsang Rinpoché, the man who headed the search party, and he filled in for the other two whenever either was away.

Although Tibetan studies ignore all things scientific, traditional education maintained a high intellectual and moral standard in Tibet for centuries. The Tibetan student was presented with a broad spectrum of knowledge, from reading and writing to memorization, dance and music, astrology, poetry, and composition. Higher studies included Sanskrit, the art of healing, arts and crafts, metaphysics, dialectics, and the philosophy of religion.

Tibetan children typically begin, as did the Dalai Lama, by learning to read and write by copying. First, he learned the Tibetan form of printing and memorized one verse of scripture every day. At eight years old, he learned the ordinary written form of Tibetan through his teacher, who wrote the Tibetan characters in chalk dust on a chalkboard. The Dalai Lama would then copy over the letter in chalk. Only after eight months of study and improved proficiency was he allowed to write on paper. With few trees in Tibet, paper was used with strict economy.

Only after learning the mechanics of writing Tibetan were the elements of grammar and spelling introduced. All told, the whole process of learning to write well took about five years. Although learning to read and write is, in itself, an important and worthwhile endeavor, Tibetans' main purpose in education is as a means of studying Buddhist scripture. The Buddhist philosophy fuels all within the Buddhist day.

The Dalai Lama's daily schedule began at 6 A.M., when he would rise, dress, and pray for an hour. After seven, his breakfast was carried to him, usually consisting of a bowl of tsampa, with caramel or honey, and tea. His studies began shortly thereafter.

The Dalai Lama's classroom was a veranda next to his bedroom. Although it was cold, the room had adequate light by which to study. He remembers being amused hearing an old monk in the room next door chanting, falling asleep during his mantra, and waking up again to continue.

Trying to ignore his impulse to disregard his studies, the Dalai Lama began his scholarly day with penmanship, and then went on to memorization. At ten o'clock he had a break, during which he attended governmental meetings. He was expected to participate in these meetings from the day of his installation, although he was too young to discern their import. The meetings took place in the Potala in a room next to his bedroom, and after they ended, he returned to his veranda for more studies.

During this period, his junior tutor came to hear the passage of scripture that he had memorized earlier that day. His teacher would read and explain the next passage, which he was to learn the following day, and at noon, a bell was rung and a conch blown. This signaled not only midday but also playtime for the Dalai Lama.

The boy had many wonderful toys to amuse him, owing to his station in life and the many foreign governments who sent gifts for his pleasure. U.S. President Franklin D. Roosevelt contributed a gold watch and a pair of songbirds; the British sent a metal building set; and Indian officials sent toys they had imported from distant nations. Among his prized possessions were a clockwork train and a set of lead soldiers. The Chinese gift, bolts of silk, was not remotely interesting to a small boy and did not impress him.

Shortly after one o'clock, the Dalai Lama ate a light lunch before embarking on his afternoon studies. By then, the afternoon sun had crested and shadow bathed his study area, which did nothing to enhance his enthusiasm for further study. His tutors often chastised him for dawdling, but he eventually resumed study in various subjects with his junior tutor. Afterward, they discussed the elements of debate—an activity that is central to the Tibetan monk's life.

At four, tea was served. In Tibet, the quality of tea produced is highly dependent on the quality of the butter used in its preparation. In the Potala, where butter was fresh and creamy, the tea was of high quality, and the Dalai Lama enjoyed it very much.

FINDING IT DIFFICULT TO BE HOLY

When teatime was over, the Dalai Lama practiced debating with two monks until about five-thirty, when the day's studies ended. At that time, the Dalai Lama bolted to the roof and his telescope. Aside from the magnificent view of the Himalayas, which he could see from the palace's rooftop vantage, the Dalai Lama enjoyed watching prisoners in the state facility of Shöl, the village at the foot of the Potala. He felt as if the prisoners there were his friends, and he monitored their activities closely as they walked about in the compound. Whenever the prisoners spied him, they immediately threw themselves down in prostration. This vexed the boy, so he took care not to let the prisoners see him.

The Dalai Lama sometimes fell into trouble when his observations ended. From the east window, he spied on novice monks, and was astounded by what he saw—monks shirking responsibility, cutting classes, and even fighting. In his autobiography, he recalls telling himself that these monks were extremely stupid, and when the violence became too ugly, he turned away.

From the west window, he saw out into the marketplace, which a visitor described this way:

> The inner town is composed of nothing but stores. Shops extend in unbroken lines and the dealers overflow into the street. There are no shop windows in our sense of the word. One finds numbers of general stores containing a large range of goods from needles to rubber boots; near them smart shops selling draperies and silks. Provision stores contain, as well as local produce, American corned beef, Australian butter, and English whisky. There is nothing one cannot buy, or at least order.[5]

Yet again the Dalai Lama had to watch covertly, lest the shoppers spot him. When that happened, everyone in the crowd would run over and prostrate before his window. He remembers how he boyishly rewarded them: "I remember blowing bubbles of spit which fell on to several people's heads as they threw themselves down to the ground far below!"[6]

Although considered a god, the boy was obviously human and even admits to stealing within the palace. From his vantage point he sometimes saw items in the marketplace that he wanted, but he had no money. At these times, he would steal change from pilgrims' offerings in the temple and send someone from the palace to go out and buy the objects he desired, since the only times he left the Potala was to go to Norbulingka in the spring, and to attend some festivals. Even then, he was carried in a palanquin and never able to wander about freely on his own.

When the Dalai Lama was nine, he discovered two hand-crank movie projectors and some rolls of film among the possessions of the Thirteenth Dalai Lama. Yet no one—including the Dalai Lama—had any idea how to operate them. Finally, he found an old Chinese monk who had been entrusted to the care of the Thirteenth Dalai Lama when he was a boy and still lived in the Potala. Although kind and sincere, he had a very bad temper, but he proved to be a good technician and helped the boy operate the movie projector. From then on, movies enthralled the Dalai Lama, and he quickly learned to operate the machinery himself. However, his film store, left by the Thirteenth Dalai Lama, was limited to documentaries, such as the coronation of King George V of Great Britain and a film about gold mining. He enjoyed them nonetheless and watched them repeatedly.

After a period of such activities, the Dalai Lama sometimes ate his evening meal with one or more of his sweepers or with some monks from Namgyal monastery, the Dalai Lama's own monastery, housed inside the Potala. Most often, however, he ate with his Masters of the Kitchen, Robes, and Ritual and sometimes his chief of staff. This communal meal gave him a feeling of kinship, which he craved.

Later, the Dalai Lama went down to the courtyard, where he was to pray while walking. Instead of praying, he often created stories in his head or thought about those he had heard at bedtime. At nine o'clock, the Dalai Lama's day ended.

During this time in the Dalai Lama's life, Lobsang Samten was sent away to a private school. The Dalai Lama speculates that this was done because they fought so often. Losing Lobsang Samten as a playmate was a major blow; yet, this first loss was minimal compared to what he would come to lose in the future.

NOTES

1. Diki Tsering, *Dalai Lama, My Son*, p. 108.

2. Tenzin Gyatso, *Freedom in Exile*, p. 21.

3. Thubten Jigme Norbu and Heinrich Harrer, *Tibet Is My Country* (London: Wisdom Publications, 1986), p. 171.

4. Quoted in Mary Craig, *Kundun*, p. 85.

5. Heinrich Harrer, *Seven Years in Tibet* (Los Angeles: Jeremy P. Tarcher, 1953), p. 147.

6. Tenzin Gyatso, *Freedom in Exile*, p. 44.

Chapter 5

THE CHINESE INVASION

By ten years of age, the Dalai Lama's life was an endless course of education and ritual. His studies continued as they had, without interruption, and a majority of his time was spent in one palace or another, depending upon the season. Although intelligent people naturally crave opportunities for new experiences and adventures, the Dalai Lama was severely restricted by Tibet's isolationist status in the world and its deep-seated religious traditions, which included strict protocol regarding his behavior. He was a virtual prisoner of his society. The world outside Lhasa compelled him, and he wanted change in his structured existence.

Still too young to implement the changes he desired, he amused himself with available diversions. One of the Dalai Lama's greatest passions became three automobiles, which had been left by the Thirteenth Dalai Lama—a 1931 Dodge and two 1927 Baby Austins (British motor cars). The cars had been carried in pieces over the Himalayas and then reassembled once they reached Lhasa; however, the vehicles had never been driven, due to the lack of motor roads in the city. The boy found them fascinating, and spent many hours with a mechanic, putting the cars back in working order.

About this time, the Dalai Lama's formal studies transitioned into dialectical discussion, or logical debate. This involved memorization of lengthy Buddhist treatises, and debate with learned scholars. His interest in intellectual studies had grown since his youngest days as a student, and his tutors reveled in his progress. Along with his passion for higher knowledge of the spiritual world, his interest in the secular world also continued to grow. At times, his instructors were stunned by questions he presented to them for which they had no answers. The Dalai Lama read newspapers, such as Tibet's *Mirror* and the *Illustrated London News,* which was sent to him by British representatives in Tibet. They also sent him magazines with picture captions translated to Tibetan, such as *Life.* The Thirteenth Dalai Lama had also left a set of illustrated books in English about World War I, which he had translated into Tibetan. Using these originals along-side the translations, the Fourteenth Dalai Lama had begun to teach him-self English. He found the study difficult and hoped for a better teacher. The mentor he sought was on his way.

In September 1939, just before the Dalai Lama had arrived in Lhasa, Britain declared war on Germany, and within hours, Indian soldiers had detained Austrian mountaineer Heinrich Harrer, who had been hiking in the Himalayas. Although Harrer and his party were not soldiers, the British saw the men as potential enemies. The Indian military arrested them and remanded them to an internment camp near Bombay, India.

After several unsuccessful escape attempts, Harrer finally managed to flee with a group of companions, including Peter Aufschnaiter, on April 29, 1944. Harrer and Aufschnaiter settled on a quest for the "Forbidden City" of Lhasa, where few white men had been permitted to travel. Trekking to Lhasa would help them avoid recapture by Indian soldiers as well, as it was nestled deep in the Himalayas, where few traveled.

After twenty months' journeying, they reached Lhasa on January 15, 1946, and had little trouble penetrating Tibetan defenses. Bearded and wearing stained woolen trousers, torn shirts, greasy sheepskin cloaks, and shabby boots, they appeared to be more Tibetan than European.

Although Harrer and Aufschnaiter enjoyed the Tibetan people, who they found to be warm and friendly, they were appalled by the lack of san-itation in Lhasa and hoped to avoid any serious illnesses during their stay. The Tibetan practice was to defecate in public trenches, and to urinate wherever convenient. Packs of mangy dogs roamed the city, and were not always docile. Yet the men were intent on remaining in the foreign land, and learning what they could about the Tibetan culture. Because of their cosmopolitan background, they were able to perform tasks Tibetans had not even conceived of, and became involved with many civil projects dur-ing their stay, including building irrigation canals, gardening, news gath-ering, and mapmaking.

The Dalai Lama scoped the activities of the foreign visitors through his rooftop telescope at the Potala and was intrigued. The strangers had al-ready met his parents and become friends with his brother, Lobsang Samten, who had returned to Lhasa by this time. As the members of his family, abbots from individual monasteries, and his servants were the only people who had the right to speak with the Dalai Lama directly, he depended on Lobsang Samten to bring him the local news each week. He had myriad questions about the outsiders and delighted in Lobsang Samten's tales of their adventures.

TIBETANS AND THE WORLD

In 1947, Tibetan news took on an international flavor, and not all of the reports were good. In March, the Inter-Asian Relations Conference convened in India to assess the status of Asia in the period following World War II. At this gathering, Tibet was represented as an independent nation, as evidenced by the country's delineation on a conference map and the first appearance of the Tibetans' newly designed national flag. The Chinese were furious, and rejected these symbols of Tibetan independence, claiming that Tibet was still part of China. They formally complained to the organizers of the conference and the map was removed, though the flag on the delegation's table was permitted to remain. The simple act of removing the map was not only a patent indication of China's greater power and status in the world, but pointed to India's future posture on Tibet.

China did not intend to allow Tibet to stand alone, although Tibetans claim China had never been a true ruler of Tibet in the past. Most recently, China had again taken up the patron position in 1914, during the Simla Convention. Great Britain had acted as mediator, to settle border disputes between Tibet and China after the break-up of the Qing dynasty, the declaration of Tibetan independence by the Thirteenth Dalai Lama, and his banishment of all Chinese from Tibetan soil.

An anthropologist and Tibetan historian has explained the Simla Agreement between China and Tibet this way:

> The final draft of the Simla Convention therefore declared that Tibet would be autonomous from China, but also acknowledged Chinese suzerainty over Tibet. Tibetans would administrate Tibet with its own officials in accordance with it own customs and laws, and China would not be permitted to station large numbers of troops or officials in Tibet—but China could maintain a commissioner in Lhasa and an escort of up to three hundred men.[1]

China did not agree to the convention, and no representatives were sent. Tibet had acted completely on its own behalf since that time; however, the actions taken by the Chinese at the 1947 Inter-Asian Relations Conference made Tibetan officials wonder if China intended to reclaim Tibet in the future.

However, the danger did not appear to be imminent. China was embroiled in a bloody civil war between Chinese Nationalists and the communist People's Liberation Army (PLA) of Mao Zedong. Although Tibetans were not concerned about immediate, direct military action, the mere threat of Communism terrified them. Buddhism was more than just a religion in Tibet; it was a way of life. Tibetans feared the atheistic Communists would completely change their world.

Lhasans might not have been so fearful had the Chinese not made their way back into Tibet, on a nominal level, in 1934. General Huang Musung arrived in Tibet as a representative of General Jiang Jie-shi, the leader of Nationalist China, presumably to pay respects to the departed Thirteenth Dalai Lama; however, he was given another mission—to bring Tibet back into the family of China. He presented the Dalai Lama's cabinet with a proposal that made Tibet a part of China, guaranteed Tibet's defense, and reestablished the office of amban—the Chinese representative—in Lhasa. The Chinese say the Tibetans agreed to this offer, while the Tibetans say they rejected it. Musung left Tibet, lamenting their lack of agreement, yet he was permitted to leave a Chinese representative behind to operate a radio, left to facilitate communications between Tibet and China. By agreeing to this, the Tibetans allowed the Chinese to reestablish a foothold in Tibet.

When the Tibetan government established a Foreign Affairs Bureau in 1942, the Chinese saw the move as daring, and when Tibet refused to allow even pack animals to carry supplies meant for the Chinese army through Tibet, it almost brought them to war. Chinese troops moved to the border, but the British facilitated another compromise. Once the Chinese promised noninterference and to transport only nonmilitary items, the Tibetans capitulated, the supply routes were opened, and the conflict cooled.

Tibetans, however, knew how vulnerable their country was to a Chinese attack, and a few years later, officials decided to send a delegation on a world tour, hoping to gain alliances with other nations. Tibet's finance secretary led the mission, which included a monk, a merchant, and the son of a foreign minister. The group would visit India, China, San Francisco, the Philippines, Hawaii, and a few European countries to determine the business climate and learn how Tibet could establish relations with the countries' leaders.

But while Tibet was trying to establish an international presence, the Dalai Lama suffered a personal loss—the sudden death of his father. Choekyong Tsering had gone to visit one of his estates and come back with severe abdominal pain. After a month of suffering and wasting away, he died. It was speculated that he was a victim of political intrigue and poisoning, since he was in otherwise good health and only forty-seven years old.

The Dalai Lama would miss his father, but for him, death was merely transition. He was confident that his father's spirit would return, according to his Buddhists beliefs. The Dalai Lama did not have, however, the strong attachment to his parents that a normal child would have, as he spent so little time around them. As a result, he was spared the overwhelming grief of such a loss. Right before his father died, his tutor had actually forbidden him from going to his parents' house, feeling that the family's influence was negatively affecting the young monk's behavior.

Unlike the Dalai Lama, the rest of the family was devastated over Choekyong Tsering's death, although not all members of the family were present at the time. Gyalo Thondup and Tsering Dolma's husband were in Taiwan. However, Tsering Dolma and her children had joined her parents in Lhasa by that time, and two more children had been born to Diki Tsering—Jetsun Pema, in 1940, and Tendzin Choegyal, in 1946. Thubten Jigme Norbu and Lobsang Samten were also visiting in Lhasa when their father died. Jetsun Pema recalls, "I was still very young at the time, but I could feel an infinite sadness hanging over the house."[2]

After two days of praying, Choekyong Tsering was cremated, and a forty-nine-day period of mourning took place, as is the Tibetan custom. His ashes were later taken back to Kumbum by Thubten Jigme Norbu and buried at Kumbum monastery.

INTERNAL STRUGGLES AND OUTSIDE INFLUENCE

While the Tibetan delegation was abroad, the royal family still mourned, and political troubles soon arose. Some insist that Choekyong Tsering's involvement in a political plot may be how he met his untimely demise. "I'm quite certain my father was murdered," said Gyalo Thondup.[3] It all stemmed from the family's continued closeness with the former regent, Reting Rinpoché, who had brought the Dalai Lama to power.

Citing an unlucky year as predicted by his astrologers, Reting Rinpoché had taken a sabbatical from his duties in Lhasa in 1941. He had planned to take a pilgrimage to India and return when the year was over. During his absence, he willingly handed the reins of government over to Tathag Rinpoché, an ostensibly forbidding man, in his seventies. Heinrich Harrer remarked: "Strict and severe in the performance of his duties, he has as many enemies as friends."[4] Yet he had been junior tutor to the Dalai Lama, who found him to be warm and kind. But in politics, perception is everything.

Tathag Rinpoché's regime may have seemed stringent in comparison to the previous regent's, since Reting Rinpoché's term of regency was one of lax ethics. Although he was a monk who took a vow of celibacy, Reting Rinpoché was involved with married women. He also used his position to gain monetary advantage. He owned one of Tibet's three largest trading companies, which was renowned for inappropriate trading practices. Alarmed at so much corruption in the government, Tathag Rinpoché reluctantly took control, and vowed to return integrity to the position.

In 1947, Reting Rinpoché tried to regain his place as regent. A bomb, disguised as a present for Tathag Rinpoché, exploded before reaching its target, and Reting Rinpoché's plan to enlist Nationalist China's help in regaining control of the country was exposed.

Tathag Rinpoché acted swiftly and sent a military contingent to arrest the former regent and take him to the Potala for questioning. When the monks of Reting Rinpoché's Sera monastery heard the news, they revolted and began shooting in the streets of Lhasa. In return, the government bombarded the monastery with cannons, troops overpowered the Sera monks, and peace was restored in twelve days' time. Reting Rinpoché was put into the Potala prison, where he, too, mysteriously died in less than a week.

Still too young to completely understand what had happened, the Dalai Lama regretted the loss of his father and his former tutor and went on with his life. In 1948, when he was thirteen, he was formally admitted to the large monasteries of Ganden, Drepung, and Sera. For this, he was required to attend and participate in debates with the abbots of Drepung's three colleges and Sera's two.

Although the boy was nervous, he seemed to relax once inside the monasteries, feeling as if he had been at those places and had done the same things before. After the debates, the high lamas told him he had passed to their satisfaction, and the Dalai Lama was spurred to further exercise his intellect and spirit to make them grow stronger.

His interest in all things Western flourished, as well. Although two of the three cars left by the Thirteenth Dalai Lama were again drivable, he was not permitted to go near them. However, any boy might find the same attraction to such vehicles, and their pull was too strong for even a Dalai Lama to ignore.

His driver had the keys to the other vehicles, so the Dalai Lama selected the working Baby Austin, which started with a hand crank, and revved the engine. After easing the car out of the garage, he proceeded to take a spin around the garden. Before getting very far, however, the car smashed into one of the Norbulingka's numerous trees.

Horrified by what he had done, the Dalai Lama worked quickly to remedy his predicament. He managed to get the car back into the garage, and tried to repair the broken headlight. He found a piece of glass that fit properly into the place where the broken glass had been, but then realized that the broken glass had been tinted. He smeared the newly restored glass with sugar syrup in order to match the original, and it worked perfectly. "But even so, I felt extremely guilty when I next saw my driver. I felt sure that he must know, or at least that he would find out, what had happened. But he never said a word."[5]

During most days, the preteen Dalai Lama stayed out of trouble. He was embroiled in complex studies, although none of them involved government or world politics, which was shortsighted in view of his impending political responsibilities. Yet his curiosity about everything was boundless, and he still relied on his telescope as a link to the outside world—and on his influence whenever he saw fit.

He was both delighted and disappointed by the stories Lobsang Samten told him about the two Austrians, who had been "knife walking"—ice skating. Because of the position of the lake to the telescope, the Dalai Lama could not see their activities, which he found thoroughly frustrating. Through Lobsang Samten, he solved the problem. Harrer wrote, "He would have dearly liked to see us disporting ourselves on the ice, but as that was impossible he sent me his moving picture camera with instruction to film the rink and the skaters for him."[6] Harrer was so successful that the Dalai Lama asked Harrer to film Tibetan festivals and Buddhist ceremonies around Lhasa as well, and provided Harrer with precise instructions as to what he wanted filmed.

THUNDER IN THE EAST

Outside Tibet, world events were brewing. General Jiang Jie-shi and the Kuomintang succumbed to the People's Liberation Army (PLA) of Mao Zedong in January of 1949, inciting greater fear of the Communists in the hearts of Tibetans.

Aside from Sino-Tibetan history to make them nervous about Chinese intervention, Tibetans knew that Chinese Communist spies lived and worked in their country in the guise of monks and traders, with a mission to determine the strength of the Tibetan army and the extent of aid they were receiving from foreign powers. To alleviate tensions, the cabinet voted to expel all Chinese citizens from Tibet in July 1949.

Communist China perceived the act as aggression, whereby Tibet again promoted itself as an independent nation—precisely what the Tibetans wanted to imply. By expelling the Chinese, Tibet wanted China to know that they did not intend to fall in line with Communist philosophy.

Chinese leaders blamed the British—the so-called imperialists—for this new Tibetan assertiveness. Shortly after the Chinese representative was permitted to stay in Tibet in 1934, the Tibetans had also agreed to a British foreign office in Lhasa. Although neither authorization was intended as more than a step toward establishing international relations, the Chinese saw Britain's presence as "imperialist intervention," owing to the claim China had on Tibet. To make matters worse, Tibet allowed Britain to maintain a foreign office even after the Chinese expulsion.

Tibetan leaders were further encouraged when, in the second half of 1949, the Tibetan world-tour party returned to Tibet. With them, they brought new buyers for Tibetan products; information on agricultural and other machinery; and a dismantled Jeep, which the Dalai Lama's mechanic reassembled for him. The Tibetan government was well pleased in its treatment by the foreign entities, especially the United States. The party had toured machine factories in the United States and had been treated with the respect due any other independent nation.

By then, the Dalai Lama—who was fourteen years old—was expert in religion, metaphysics, and all things spiritual. Although he had a strong interest in the world outside Lhasa, he was still uninvolved in the day-to-day workings of the country's administration.

During this period, the Dalai Lama was most interested in movies. He loved the films that Heinrich Harrer had made for him, and consequently asked the Austrian to build him a movie house. For the first time, the gates of the Norbulingka's inner garden were open to a westerner. Harrer described the Dalai Lama's sanctuary this way:

> The peach and pear blossoms were in full bloom. Peacocks strutted proudly through the grounds and hundreds of rare plants stood in pots in the sunshine.
>
> In addition to the temples there were many small houses scattered about under the trees. Each was used for a special purpose—one was for meditation, another for reading and study, and others served as meeting places for the monks. The largest building, several stories high, stood in the center of the garden and was half a temple and half a residence for His Holiness.[7]

The Dalai Lama was not in residence while Harrer built his theater, however. Their first meeting occurred when the Dalai Lama called upon him to install a movie reel in the projector. Immediately upon meeting the Austrian, the young ruler nicknamed him "yellow head," instantly posed a series of questions, and asked Harrer to instruct him in all things Western, including the English language. Harrer agreed, and for the first time, an "outsider" was able to speak with the Dalai Lama, face-to-face. This was very significant, and a precursor to the Dalai Lama's attitude of accessibility, which directly contradicted Tibetan protocol.

Many traditions were broken through the friendship of the Dalai Lama and Heinrich Harrer. One custom dictated that everyone sit in a lower position than the Dalai Lama, but Harrer was able to sit beside him. No one was supposed to look the Dalai Lama in the eye, yet Harrer became the Dalai Lama's closest confidant. "He seems to me like a person who had for years brooded in solitude over different problems, and now that he had at last someone to talk to, wanted to know all the answers at once."[8] Harrer had to study to keep up with the Dalai Lama's questions, and spent some part of each afternoon instructing him in matters related to the outside world. Their closeness lasted until Tibet became too dangerous—for both of them.

OMINOUS PORTENTS

In 1949, Tibetans believed that ominous signs pointed to imminent trouble. A bright horse-tailed comet appeared during that year and remained in the nighttime sky for weeks. Tibetans had not forgotten the 1947 predictions of the state oracle, who prophesied that in 1950, Tibet would face "great difficulty." After the appearance of the comet, people began to think about gathering their assets and leaving the country.

Tibetans were very concerned that a new Chinese invasion was about to occur, just like the one that had taken place in 1910, after the appearance of a similar comet. At that time, the Chinese army, along with the Qing dynasty, fell apart. This time, Lhasans were not so sure that Tibetans would prevail against the Communists. The Tibetan government decided to prepare for the inevitable and pursued internal reforms, assessed possibilities for external aid, and even attempted détente with the Red Chinese.

In accordance with these plans, they took stock of their army, and found it to be only 8,500 soldiers strong. This, in comparison to the millions of Chinese, was no army at all. They had enough rifles, but their heavier artillery, including mortars and machine guns, were fewer than 500 in number. The Tibetan army had never been intended as a fighting army, only as a police force and a vehicle for keeping out unauthorized travelers. The National Assembly knew that there was no way Tibet could fight a war with such limited resources, and set out to improve the army and its borders. The outer province of Kham[9] strengthened its border with China, and to improve communications, the Tibetan government hired Robert Ford—a British national who had been constructing Tibet's first radio broadcasting station, Radio Lhasa—to extend the network of wireless communication to Chamdo, the largest city in that region.

The Tibetan government also opted to enlist the help of the countries previously visited by the Tibetan trade and industry delegation. This time, four delegations were appointed to travel to Britain, the United States, India, and Nepal, to seek assistance in persuading China to halt any attacks on Tibet. Before the parties left, communications were sent to each of the countries, outlining the perceptible threat and asking the governments to receive the Tibetan delegations in good faith.

Yet replies to these communiqués were disheartening. Britain and the United States pushed the question into the lap of India, which had been closely allied with Tibet since the reign of the Thirteenth Dalai Lama. India, saying it had not received any request, refused to act, and even indicated a desire to deny involvement in the Tibetan situation entirely, since they had just come through a war for independence from Great Britain.

Although the British had already supplied guns and ammunition to Tibet, they no longer had an interest in the region. They responded that the distance between Great Britain and Tibet was too wide to offer military support. The United States replied along the same lines and further refused to receive the delegation, stating that any such action could speed Chinese military action in Tibet, owing to Communist sentiments so strongly opposed to capitalist intervention.

India ultimately relented and provided arms and ammunition to Tibet, in addition to training for new Tibetan recruits. Yet India continued to refuse direct military assistance and cited the Simla Agreement of 1914. As Simla included provisions for Tibet's protection from Chinese aggression, the Indian government deemed that Tibet was obligated to open negotiations with China for a peaceful settlement.

In November 1949, the Tibetans took India's advice and wrote to Chairman Mao, asking that the Chinese respect the independence of Tibet, and included the request: "In view of the fact that Chinghai [Qinghai] and Sikiang [Xikang], etc. are being situated on the border of Tibet, we would like to have an assurance that no Chinese troops would cross the Tibetan frontier from the Sino-Tibetan border, or any such Military action."[10] The Tibetans never received a reply.

THE DRAGON BREATHES FIRE

On New Year's Day 1950, just three months after the Communist takeover of China, Lhasans heard on Radio Peking that the People's Liberation Army intended also to "liberate" Taiwan, Hainan,[11] and Tibet. They insisted that Tibet had fallen under the influence of foreign imperialists and required emancipation to secure China's western borders. The Tibetans were now sure that their earlier qualms had been justified. Their time was running out.

By late 1949, much of Amdo had already been secured by the Red Chinese. As there was no means of communication between Amdo and Lhasa, however, this fact went unnoticed in the capital city. Lhasans continued to worry about the city around them, and lived under the impression that it would be years before the Chinese actually came their way. Daily life continued in and around Lhasa as it had for centuries.

In May 1950, Radio Peking announced the takeover of Hainan, saying that only Taiwan and Tibet were still in need of liberation. The Chinese offered the Tibetans "regional autonomy" and said that if the Tibetans agreed to peaceful submission, they would guarantee religious freedom.

With no immediate reply from Lhasa, the PLA launched their first attack in Kham within a few days, and took the city of Dengkog. Two weeks later, seven hundred fierce Kham warriors retook the city and slaughtered every Chinese soldier, about six hundred in all.

Still oblivious to the ferocity of battles taking place in the east, the Lhasans suffered an unanticipated blow. On August 15, while the Dalai Lama was at the Norbulingka eating dinner, an earthquake with a magnitude of 8.6 struck Assam, in the northeastern corner of India, with tremors so violent that they shook the earth as far as Calcutta, 777 miles away. The sound from its aftershocks traveled twelve hundred miles, all the way to Tibet's western borders. Tibetans feared that Sera monastery in the eastern part of Tibet had been shelled, and saw the earthquake as a portent of evil, signaling that their world was about to end. And so it was.

On October 7, the first and second field armies of China, composed of 84,000 soldiers, crossed the Yangtze River, invaded Kham at dawn, and fought their way to Chamdo. When news of the approaching Chinese hit the city, there was panic. Everyone set to praying, consulting fortunetellers, stringing fresh prayer flags, and making prostrations, in hopes of solving the problem through the power of prayer. The Dalai Lama said, "But believing the country would be saved without human effort, through prayers alone, resulted from limited knowledge. From this point of view religious sentiment actually became an obstacle."[12]

When Ngabo Ngawang Jigme, the governor of Chamdo, heard the Chinese were only a day away, he radioed Lhasa for permission to surrender. When it was denied, he disguised himself as a junior officer and fled the city. The people went wild with fear and rage when they learned of his flight the following day. It was inconceivable that he had made no preparations for the people or his troops but had abandoned them, hoping to preserve his own safety. One week later, the People's Republic of China (PRC) formally announced on Radio Peking that they had entered Tibet in order to perform its liberation.

On November 7, the then desperate Tibetan government appealed to the United Nations for support. However, Tibet had never become a member of the organization, and its pleas went unheard. The people then began to clamor for the Dalai Lama to take political control of the country. He seemed to be their only means of unity and hope.

Not wanting to assume the throne for fear that he was not yet ready, the Dalai Lama called in the Gadong oracle. After ceremonial rites were performed and the medium had assumed the spirit of his protective god, he came before the Dalai Lama, laid a kata across his lap, and said, "His time has come."[13]

This pronouncement set a quiet terror in the heart of the young Dalai Lama, then only fifteen years old. He naturally hesitated to assume such a huge burden at such a young age, especially since he had not been sufficiently prepared to take control, but the Dalai Lama quickly recognized his importance to the people and the country. Although his investiture would be three years earlier than tradition dictated, he agreed to become the supreme temporal ruler of Tibet on November 17. "I could not refuse my responsibilities," he wrote. "I had to shoulder them, put my boyhood behind me and immediately prepare myself to lead my country."[14]

Two weeks before the ceremony, the Dalai Lama got word that Thubten Jigme Norbu, by then abbot of Kumbum monastery, was on his way to Lhasa. Upon his arrival, the Dalai Lama noticed that he was haggard, and wondered what sort of stress he had been in.

The Dalai Lama's brother explained that Kumbum was under Communist control. He had been kept as a virtual prisoner at Kumbum, as had his monks. The Communists insisted that they accept Communist ideals. Thubten Jigme Norbu was only released under the condition that he travel to Lhasa and attempt to convert the Dalai Lama to the Communist way of life. He wrote, "Should the Dalai Lama resist the march of progress, they indicated, ways and means would have to be found to get rid of him. At this point they even let me see quite clearly that if necessary they would regard fratricide as justifiable in the circumstances if there remained no other way of advancing the cause of Communism."[15]

Thubten Jigme Norbu did not intend to kill his brother, but came to warn him of the grave danger he faced. The Chinese knew how much faith the Tibetan people put in the Dalai Lama, and viewed him as a threat to the promotion of Communist ideals. Thubten Jigme Norbu pretended to go along with the plan, in order to relay the situation awaiting all of Tibet if the Chinese took control. He warned the Dalai Lama that the Chinese were not only atheistic but also opposed to the practice of religion in any form.

By that time, Thubten Jigme Norbu had decided that even Buddhists have reason for violence, and so renounced his monastic vows. He begged his brother to leave Tibet. His own intention was to escape the country and try to make contact with the Americans. He was sure that under the circumstances, they would support the principle of a free Tibet, if only to stop the spread of Communism.

But nothing would halt the Tibetans' desire for the god-king to take the throne. They saw the Dalai Lama as protector of Tibet and their salvation. On the morning of November 17, the Dalai Lama prepared for his investiture. He dressed in his finest clothes, and his Master of the Robes handed him a green cloth to tie around his waist, as astrologers had deemed green to be his auspicious color. He went to the chapel, and before all the members of government, he received the Golden Wheel, symbolizing his assumption of political power.

His first order was to release every prisoner at Shöl prison, those men whom he had considered his friends from years of observation from afar. He then appointed two prime ministers—one layman and one monk. The appointment of one religious person and one nonreligious person is customary with all government posts in Tibet, reaching back to the time of the Great Fifth, who desired a balance of religion and state. The Dalai Lama chose two strong men, recognizing his own deficiencies in matters of state.

The Dalai Lama also decided to try for international support once again, and to this end, he sent delegations to the United States, Great Britain, and Nepal. Although Tibet had been rebuffed more than once, he thought it was imperative to try to obtain outside assistance in negotiating a Communist withdrawal of forces. Also to this end, he sent a fourth delegation, directly to China.

At the end of 1950, the National Assembly agreed that the Dalai Lama should move to southern Tibet with his senior government officials. Wanting to protect their leader, they thought this relocation would allow him the option of slipping quickly over the border into India if the situation became too dangerous.

Many baggage trains were sent ahead, one of them carrying boxes of treasure—gold and silver from the vaults at the Potala. All of the preparations were made in secret, for fear that the people of Lhasa would learn of the Dalai Lama's plans and become alarmed.

Yet Tibetans would not have been upset that he was escaping. On the contrary, they would be pleased to know that he would remain alive and free. To Tibetans, the Dalai Lama is Tibet, and his demise would surely mean the downfall of the whole country and the Tibetan way of life. By keeping his departure secret, officials hoped to deter any group demonstrations, in which Tibetans might be hurt or killed.

The Dalai Lama left the two prime ministers in charge of the government in Lhasa and, with his traveling party, left the city at night. He was headed for Yadong, just inside the border with Sikkim, to the southwest of the Tibetan capital. On January 4, 1951, after ten days' travel, the party reached their destination.

Not long after their arrival, they received dire news from the delegations sent abroad. All had been turned away; only the delegation to China had reached its destination. The Dalai Lama was finally convinced that Tibet would have to face the Chinese alone.

With no other options, talks had to be arranged with the Chinese. But before a committee could be formed, the Dalai Lama received a report on Chamdo from Ngabo Ngawang Jigme, who had been captured by the Chinese and later released to resume his position as governor of Chamdo, although the Chinese were clearly in control. He suggested that the only option was for the Tibetans to negotiate peacefully, and volunteered to lead a team into Beijing. Not knowing that the governor had deserted his people and believing him to be a shrewd negotiator, the Dalai Lama agreed, and sent along two officials from his party in Yadong and two from Lhasa to accompany him.

In the spring, the Dalai Lama hoped that the delegation in Beijing would bring good news, yet did not expect it. Still, nothing prepared him for the shock of what he heared in a June broadcast on Radio Beijing: the Seventeen-Point Agreement for the Peaceful Liberation of Tibet had been signed by the People's Republic of China and the "local" government of Tibet.

No authorization had been given for such an agreement. Certainly the Tibetan representatives in Beijing possessed no authority to entitle them to binding a contract with the Chinese. He could do nothing but hope the agreement was kind to Tibet.

On the surface, some clauses of the Seventeen-Point Agreement seemed beneficial. The fourth clause stated that the central authorities would not alter the existing political system in Tibet and that the powers of the Dalai Lama would not diminish. Clause seven guaranteed religious freedom. Clause eleven prohibited coercion from the central government to carry out reforms, and put the power with the local government. Clause thirteen stated that the People's Liberation Army would not take "a single needle or thread" from the people of Tibet. However, the first clause of the Seventeen-Point Agreement was most damaging. It stated, "The Tibetan people shall unite and drive out imperialist aggressive forces from Tibet; the Tibetan people shall return to the family of the motherland—the People's Republic of China."[16]

The Tibetans were astonished. They never believed themselves to be part of China, stating that China's suzerainty in the past had no ties over them in the present. Even worse, owing to the reports they had gotten from Kumbum, they worried that the very fabric of Tibetan life had begun to tear.

NOTES

1. Melvyn C. Goldstein, *The Snow Lion and the Dragon* (Berkeley, Calif.: University of California Press, 1997), p. 33.

2. Jetsun Pema, *Tibet: My Story* (Shaftsbury, Dorset, England: Element Books Limited, 1997), p. 11.

3. Quoted in Mary Craig, *Kundun*, p. 120.

4. Heinrich Harrer, *Seven Years in Tibet*, p. 189.

5. Tenzin Gyatso, *Freedom in Exile*, p. 40.

6. Harrer, *Seven Years in Tibet*, p. 254.

7. Harrer, *Seven Years in Tibet*, p. 269.

8. Harrer, *Seven Years in Tibet*, p. 273.

9. With Amdo in the north and U-Tsang in the east, Kham completed the three provinces of historical Tibet.

10. Quoted in Tsering Shakya, *The Dragon in the Land of Snows* (New York: Putnam, 1999), p. 27.

11. An island off the coast of China in the South China Sea, which had been under nationalist control before the Communist takeover of China.

12. Quoted in Avedon, *In Exile from the Land of Snows*, p. 31.

13. Tenzin Gyatso, *Freedom in Exile*, p. 53.

14. The Dalai Lama of Tibet, *My Land and My People*, p. 62.

15. Quoted in Mary Craig, *Kundin*, p. 139.

16. "The Agreement of the Central People's Government and the Local Government of Tibet on Measures for the Peaceful Liberation of Tibet," Beijing, China, 23 May 1951.

Chapter 6

DEALING WITH THE MOTHERLAND

The signing of the Seventeen-Point Agreement clearly shocked and dismayed the Tibetan government. Upon learning of it, the Dalai Lama's brothers and some of his advisors insisted that he flee the country and take residence in India. Yet due to centuries of Tibetan isolationism, many Tibetan officials had no idea what they might lose if the Communists took control of Tibet. They were adamant that the Dalai Lama remain in the country and wait for an explanation from the delegation to China, headed by Ngabo Ngawang Jigme. The cabinet immediately sent a telegram to him, asking for a full transcript of the agreement, and advised the delegation to wait in Beijing until they could weigh the agreement and consider their options.

Yet, the Chinese had other ideas. Soon after the signing of the Seventeen-Point Agreement, one half of the Tibetan delegation, including Ngabo Ngawang Jigme, left Beijing to enter Tibet via Chamdo. On June 16, Zhang Jinwu—the new Chinese representative to Tibet, and the balance of the delegation left for Tibet, via Taiwan. They would meet the Dalai Lama at Yadong and accompany him back to Lhasa in a demonstration of solidarity.

When Tibetan officials heard that a Chinese official was already en route to Tibet, they suspected the agreement was not at all beneficial to their country. They worried that Tibet had lost her autonomy and were apprehensive that the delegation had agreed to allow Chinese troops into Lhasa. They also feared that the Chinese wanted to use the Dalai Lama as a puppet to control the Tibetan people.

Tibet continued communications with the United States in hopes of gaining assistance. The United States had wanted to back Tibet in its

1950 appeal to the United Nations but had received resistance from both
India and Britain and declined to initiate any action. As a neighboring
state, newly independent India did not want to cause bad feelings with
China. Britain, having been India's parent country, had decided to back
India in its decision. Therefore, the United Nations appeal was still at a
standstill, though Tibet's chances for intervention from that arena were
not good.

By 1951, the United States had sent forces to fight in the Korean conflict and suspected that the Chinese were about to become involved in the
trouble there as well. The United States had done its best to assist nationalist China in the Chinese Civil War, and was adamant about stopping the spread of Communism. Few knew that the United States had
already offered to support Tibet behind closed doors.

A personal message, unsigned and on plain paper, was given to the
Dalai Lama by the chief of the Tibetan Foreign Affairs Bureau, who told
him it was from the United States. In it, he was reminded that Chinese
Communists preferred to gain their way through deception rather than
force, and that the establishment of a Communist representative in Lhasa
would only speed the complete takeover of Tibet. The Dalai Lama was encouraged not to return to Lhasa or to return his treasure boxes to the capital, as any treasures returned would eventually become the property of
the Communist regime.

The letter read: "If you leave Tibet, we think you should seek asylum in
India, Thailand, or Ceylon in that order of priority because then you will
be closer to Tibet and will be able to organize its resistance ... We will discuss plans and programs of military assistance and loans of money with
your representatives when you tell us who your representatives are."[1]

In American minds, the worst-case scenario would have been for the
Dalai Lama to return to Lhasa and ratify the Seventeen-Point Agree-
ment, which would repudiate Tibetan claims of Chinese aggression.
Therefore, the Americans set on a tack of trying to persuade the Dalai
Lama to renounce the accord and flee the country.

The British were skeptical of U.S. involvement in Tibet. Although
Britain was aware of the Americans' covert participation, it had agreed not
to inform India but feared that the United States was rushing to help without considering the Indian position. The British insisted that the Tibetans
had no legal right to repudiate the Seventeen-Point Agreement unless
they could prove that the delegation in Beijing had exceeded its authority
in acting on Tibet's behalf and had signed the agreement under duress.

Although it was true that Ngabo Ngawang Jigme had no direct authority to sign such a weighty agreement with the Chinese and that the

Tibetan government suspected that the delegation had been coerced, a majority of Tibetan officials still refused to repudiate the agreement without hearing what the Tibetan delegation had to say upon its return to Tibet.

Also in that pursuit, the abbots from Drepung, Sera, and Ganden monasteries arrived in Yadong and petitioned the Dalai Lama for his return to Lhasa. They said that the state oracle had been consulted on two occasions, both times instructing that the Dalai Lama should return.

MAKING A DIFFICULT DECISION

In a quandary, the Dalai Lama's foremost desire was to minimize the suffering of his people. He knew the desire for combat had increased in the people of Tibet, especially among the fierce warriors in Kham. However, not just Buddhism kept him from sanctioning war; he knew that in the face of Chinese retaliation, Tibetans had no chance.

He saw some hope in obtaining foreign help from the United States, but worried that without even speaking to the Chinese, there would be no hope for a peaceful solution. "Firstly, it was obvious to me that the most likely result of a pact with America or anyone else was war."[2] He wanted to avoid bloodshed at all costs.

The Dalai Lama also realized that the United States was on the other side of the world, while China was at Tibet's back door. Although China was not as strong as the United States monetarily, it was stronger in population by about 400 million people. He knew that any armed struggle could take a very long time and wasn't convinced that the American people would stand for losing so many citizens. If and when the United States found it necessary to pull out of Tibet, the outcome would be the same— China would be the victor. The Dalai Lama decided that it was better to try peaceful negotiations with China and save lives. "Without friends there was nothing we could do but acquiesce, submit to the Chinese dictates in spite of our strong opposition, and swallow our resentment."[3]

Although it had already been decided that he would take asylum in India on July 12, he made the last-minute decision to stay at Yadong and wait for the Chinese general.

When Zhang Jinwu arrived in Yadong, he met the Dalai Lama at Dongker Monastery. At his cadre's approach, the Dalai Lama described his feelings: "I do not know exactly what I had expected, but what I saw was three men in grey suits and peaked caps who looked extremely drab and insignificant among the splendid figures of my officials in their red and golden robes. Had I but known, the drabness was the state to which

China was to reduce us all before the end, and the insignificance was certainly an illusion."[4]

The Dalai Lama's meeting with Zhang Jinwu began with the Chinese general asking if the Dalai Lama had heard of the Seventeen-Point Agreement. After replying that he had, the Dalai Lama was handed a copy of the agreement and a declaration about China's intentions if the Dalai Lama chose to flee the country. The latter document stated that if he fled, the Dalai Lama would soon see that the Chinese had come in friendship and would then want to return to Tibet immediately. In that case, which the Chinese were certain of, they vowed to welcome him cordially.

When Zhang Jinwu asked the Dalai Lama when he would return to Lhasa, the Dalai Lama was noncommittal and simply replied, "Soon." He knew that the Chinese wished them to return to Lhasa together, to show unity; however, the Dalai Lama wanted to avoid giving such an impression. Although he would not be easily influenced by the Communists, he was less anxious after the meeting, realizing that the Chinese were men, like himself, and not the monsters his fifteen-year-old imagination had invented.

RETURNING HOME TO UNWELCOME GUESTS

After finally setting off for Lhasa, the Dalai Lama made three stops. He traveled with his old teacher Tathag Rinpoché, who had come to Yadong to provide spiritual guidance to the Dalai Lama, and who was headed back to his home monastery. Their first stop was Gyantse, where the Indian cavalry met him and offered a salute of respect. He then stopped at Samding Monastery—the home of Dorje Phagmo, a very important bodhisattva—where the leader of the monastery was a woman, the only abbess in Tibet. After stopping once more, to return Tathag Rinpoché to his monastery, the Dalai Lama arrived in Lhasa on August 18, 1951, after an eight-month absence.

At the headquarters of his bodyguard, the Dalai Lama's next meeting with General Zhang Jinwu was according to Tibetan tradition. This angered the general, who insisted he was being treated as a foreigner rather than a member of the family. He also had not liked being met *outside* the city by two members of the cabinet. Now he screamed and pounded his fist, and the Dalai Lama noticed a gold Rolex watch peeking out from under his drab grey uniform, a sign that Communist leaders were communist outside but materialist inside. The watch and Zhang Jinwu's outburst gave the Dalai Lama a better idea of the Chinese general's character, and he was pleased that he did not have to deal with him too often.

Soon after this, the Dalai Lama's older brother, Gyalo Thondup, was en route to the United States after a sixteen-month stay in Taiwan. Although the Americans offered him a scholarship to study at Stanford University, he declined, saying he wanted to get back to Tibet—a decision that surprised everyone. Thubten Jigme Norbu was already in the United States, hiding from the Communists, and told Gyalo Thondup he would be crazy to go back. But Gyalo Thondup was anxious to try to help his people and his brother, the Dalai Lama.

What Gyalo Thondup did not know was that the Chinese were entering Lhasa. On September 9, three thousand troops from the Chinese Eighteenth Army marched into the Tibetan capital. While the typical Tibetan greeting is to stick out the tongue to indicate that there are no lies on it, the people stood lining the soldiers' path, clapping—not in appreciation, but in the traditional Tibetan way of driving out evil. Children threw rocks and monks hit the soldiers with the knotted ends of their robes.

In the face of this reception, Chinese troops tried to be friendly. Loudspeakers proclaimed that they were in Lhasa to reunite the motherland and to bring progress and prosperity to Tibet. The Chinese were giving money to the monasteries and offering new titles and hefty salaries to leaders who would study Marxism and enroll their children in the new school, which the Chinese would build for them. Many forward-thinking Tibetans saw China as their country's salvation. They realized how far behind the rest of the world Tibet was and thought that China could bring them into the twentieth century.

At the end of September, the National Assembly met to consider the Sino-Tibetan bond and to discuss the Seventeen-Point Agreement; more than three hundred officials attended. Ngabo Ngawang Jigme insisted that he be allowed to explain the agreement and to clear his name of any misconduct in its signing.

In his speech to the assembly, he stated that neither he nor any members of the delegation had accepted any bribes from the Chinese. He claimed that the agreement maintained the Dalai Lama's power and would not endanger the religious and political system of his country. In closing, he said that he was willing to accept any punishment imposed if the assembly found him guilty of any wrongdoing, including a sentence of death.

After much discussion, the National Assembly advised the Dalai Lama to accept the agreement. They confirmed Ngabo Ngawang Jigme's remarks and made their formal acceptance. On October 20, 1951, a letter was drafted and a telegram sent to Mao Zedong: "The Tibet Local Government as well as the ecclesiastic and secular people unanimously support this agreement, and under the leadership of Chairman Mao and the Central People's Government, will actively support the People's Liberation Army in Tibet to consolidate national defense, drive out imperialist influences from Tibet and safeguard the unification of the territory and the sovereignty of the Motherland."[5] With that letter, Tibet became part of China.

Subsequent to the ratification of the Seventeen-Point Agreement, five thousand more troops arrived in Lhasa. However, Mao warned them to be conciliatory. He said that Tibet was slow to move and that they would have to treat Tibetans with patience.

THE CHINESE BURDEN

By the end of 1951, the population of Lhasa and its surrounding areas had nearly doubled. Chinese troops had to be fed, and their livestock—including horses, yaks, and camels—needed land for grazing. This put an enormous burden on Tibet's traditional economy.

Chinese troops put up tents in an enormous area formerly used for recreation. They also demanded a loan of two thousand tons of barley, an amount that was far beyond the ability of the state to provide. The government had to borrow the deficit from monasteries and private citizens.

With the approach of winter, tents were insufficient as housing. The Chinese began to buy land and build houses. Some Tibetan aristocrats saw this as an opportunity for profit. They sold shelter to the troops at high prices and made quick money.

Because there was no way to transport produce from China to Tibet quickly enough for it to maintain freshness, the Chinese also began to buy up land for cultivation. This angered the local peasants, especially when inflation began to take hold. Food grains became ten times as expensive as they had been before the Chinese army entered Lhasa. Butter went up nine times its price and general sundries increased by 50 to 60 percent. The people of Lhasa were on the edge of famine.

High prices were not a problem for the Chinese, who melted silver trinkets and religious ornaments and minted silver coins to be used exclusively in Tibet. Because they could be melted down and resold, the coins were acceptable to Tibetans. However, their use became so widespread that they actually helped the Chinese undermine Tibetan currency.

Propaganda was also blazoned across Lhasa and Shigatse in the form of Maoist posters and slogans. The Tibetan elite were treated to lavish state dinners and the Tibetan peasants were shown films of the People's

Liberation Army in their wars against the Kuomintang and the Japanese. The films appealed to common Tibetans, who had seen little of modern warfare, and they flocked to the cinemas, impressed by the might of the Chinese military.

One practice of the troops sent the Lhasans into a furor—the burning of animal bones for fuel inside the city. Owing to their attitude of nonviolence toward all creatures, using bones of dead animals for their own comfort was a sign of irreverence for Tibetan religious beliefs, not to mention the implications of the black, rancid smoke that filled the air as a result.

With no regard to the danger of inciting the Chinese troops to violence, Lhasan anger erupted. Children shouted slogans at the soldiers, calling them "Red Chinese Enemies of the Faith,"[6] and threw stones at them. Everyone sang songs to taunt the troops and make them look foolish, although the Chinese could not understand the words. They surmised the content of the songs by the people's laughter and raucous demeanor, and their pride was injured. They considered the abuse a loss of face—the worst insult to a Chinese person.

Zhang Jinwu came to the Dalai Lama and demanded that he issue an order for the people to stop singing and ban any criticism of his people. The Dalai Lama complied, yet despite the new laws, a popular resistance movement took root. Posters appeared, asking for the return of Tibet and of the Dalai Lama to his rightful authority. The people also demanded that Chinese troops be withdrawn. These actions angered and alarmed the Chinese further, and they demanded that the cabinet put a stop to the dissension.

An investigation was launched into the actions of the dissident group the People's Representatives, and the Chinese asked the cabinet for the names of individuals involved. They insisted that neither the Dalai Lama nor the cabinet should have any contact with the group, and demanded that the cabinet take action or they would take action themselves.

AXING TRUSTED PERSONNEL

The cabinet was under attack from both sides. While the Chinese clamored for an end to the demonstrations, Tibetans were furious over the cabinet's inability to diminish Chinese influence. One major point of contention was the absorption of Tibet's army into the People's Liberation Army, as stipulated in Article 8 of the Seventeen-Point Agreement. By March 1952, only three regiments of the Tibetan army were still intact. The other units had been disbanded, and many of the ex-soldiers had remained in Lhasa rather than return to their villages in disgrace. The remaining units were disbanded by the cabinet, rather than allowing them to be placed under Chinese command.

Unwilling to directly confront the issue, Mao Zedong wrote to the Chinese officials in Lhasa:

> Apparently not only the two Silons [prime ministers] but also the Dalai Lama and most of his clique were reluctant to accept the agreement and are unwilling to carry it out. As yet we do not have a material base for this purpose in terms of support among the masses or in the upper stratum. To force its implementation will do more harm than good. Since they are unwilling to put the agreement into effect, well then, we can leave it for the time being and wait.[7]

This was a clear indication that the Chinese saw the two prime ministers as an impediment to their administration. They were not pleased when the nonmonastic Prime Minister Lukhangwa refused their second demand for two thousand more tons of barley. He told them that the Tibetan people were simple people and produced only enough for their needs, that there was no surplus of goods, and that a surplus could not be achieved quickly. He suggested that since there would not be enough food to support the troops for more than another month or two, perhaps they should consider decreasing their forces in the city.

The Chinese employed politeness in their replies. They referred to the Seventeen-Point Agreement, which allowed them to maintain troops in Lhasa, and said, "When you can stand on your own feet, we will not stay here, even if you ask us to."[8]

Lukhangwa later pointed out that so far they had done nothing to help Tibet. If anything, they had hurt the delicate balance there, pointing to the burning of animal bones for firewood within the Holy City of Lhasa, which had done little to improve relations.

Things only worsened for Lukhangwa when he disagreed that the Tibetan flag should be removed from all military barracks and the Chinese flag raised. He told the Chinese that it was a bad idea because Tibetan troops would only take the flags down again, embarrassing the Chinese. They argued, and in the course of the heated discussion, Lukhangwa told the Chinese that it was ridiculous for them to think the Tibetans might have friendly relations with them. "If you hit a man on his head and break his skull," he said, "you can hardly expect him to be friendly."[9] The Chinese immediately closed the meeting.

During the next meeting three days later, a general of the Chinese army asked Lukhangwa if he had not been mistaken in his statements at the earlier meeting, apparently expecting an apology. Lukhangwa stood by his statement and explained that rumors of Chinese oppression in the eastern provinces of Tibet were circulating. He insisted that raising the Chinese flag would surely incite the crowds. The general became belligerent and accused Lukhangwa of imperialist influence. Lukhangwa said that if the Dalai Lama was convinced of any wrongdoing, he would give up not only his office but also his life. Zhang Jinwu stepped into the fray and said that the general was mistaken and not to take what Lukhangwa said too seriously.

Soon after the meeting, the Dalai Lama received a report from Zhang Jinwu, saying that Lukhangwa did not want to aid in Sino-Tibetan relations and suggesting that he be removed from office. He expressed the same opinion of the Dalai Lama's cabinet. When the communiqué was brought before the cabinet, they advised the Dalai Lama that conditions might improve if both prime ministers were removed from office.

Now the Dalai Lama had another difficult choice. He admired Lukhangwa's courage and did not want to give in to another Chinese imperative. Yet he realized that if he did not remove the man, his life would be in danger.

In deciding the issue, the seventeen-year-old boy put his religious training to work as his only reference point. He decided that opposition to the Chinese could only mean more strife and ultimate physical violence. As physical violence is against the Buddhist religion, he elected a course of cooperation when it was feasible and one of "passive resistance" when it was not. To avoid the possible repercussions of keeping the prime ministers in office, the Dalai Lama accepted the cabinet's recommendation and asked both to resign.

PREPARING FOR THE FUTURE

After the prime ministers had left office, the Dalai Lama took steps to further his own government by establishing a Reform Committee. One of his main ambitions was to establish a judicial system, spurred on by the mysterious death of Reting Rinpoché while in custody of the court. He also wanted to see proposals from the cabinet for a high-quality educational program. Communications also needed reform, and there was not a single road in Tibet capable of handling wheeled transport. He knew these reforms would take a long time, but he was anxious to bring Tibet into the twentieth century.

Abolishing inheritable debt was another high-priority for the Dalai Lama. In historical Tibet, debts of a father could be passed to son, grandson, and even later generations until the debt was paid. Often the lenders were landlords, who expected a share of the farmer's crops as payment. One bad harvest could send a Tibetan farmer's family into debt for years. Tibetans could also borrow from the government in times of need, and this debt passed down as well.

To remedy this injustice, the Dalai Lama abolished the principle of inheritable debt and declared amnesty on all debts owed the government. He also encouraged the cabinet to approve a plan where the government would purchase large estates from landowners and redistribute the property among people who actually lived and worked on it. This provision, however, would take some convincing, since many nobles would naturally be opposed to losing their regular incomes.

Owing to his greater involvement, and without the prime ministers to buffer relations, the Chinese began to deal more often with the Dalai Lama directly. They saw him as a seventeen-year-old, someone they could easily manipulate. He was also amenable to change whereas many older Tibetans were bound by tradition and reluctant to reform. The Chinese hoped he would see the benefit in their Communist agenda.

Yet they never realized that the Dalai Lama was beyond their often-used method of influence—bribery. As a Buddhist monk, the Dalai Lama could not be swayed by material goods or money. He only wanted the best for his people, and intelligently surveyed every option before making decisions. This meant that he sometimes viewed the Communist options as reasonable, and even small conciliations put the Chinese at ease. Eventually, tensions eased on both sides. Far from becoming a Communist, his ultimate plan was to buy time for his country, hoping to find an outside source of support in the meantime.

Gyalo Thondup had returned to Tibet in early 1952, and tried to play the same game as his younger brother—appeasing the Chinese, while hoping for an independent Tibet. To the cabinet, he pushed land reforms, but the governmental body was still not receptive. He told them, "For heaven's sake, long before my children or yours are old enough to care, the land will have been taken anyway. If you don't act now, you'll be giving the Chinese a sword with which to divide us."[10] He also backed up his words by telling the cabinet that he intended to tear up any debts owed to his own estates near the Indian border and to redistribute the land to its farmers.

Then a cable from Mao Zedong appointed Gyalo Thondup to the Chinese Youth Delegation at the World Peace Conference in Vienna. As the

Dalai Lama's brother, Gyalo Thondup saw this as an attempt at using him to convince the Tibetan people to join Communism. As they had already made Tsering Dolma chairperson of the Patriotic Association of Women, the Chinese agenda for the Dalai Lama's siblings became more obvious with Gyalo Thondup's appointment, and he was infuriated. He had no intention of becoming a Communist puppet and developed a plan to evade the request.

Pretending to be honored, Gyalo Thondup used his land-reform work as an excuse for postponing his travel to Vienna. He told Chinese officials that he had to visit his estates to make the necessary preparations. After discussing the situation with the rest of the family, Gyalo Thondup decided to seek asylum in India, in hopes of gaining outside aid for Tibet. He hurried to his estates, divided up the property, tore up the debts, and slipped over the Indian border. There he would organize the Committee for Tibetan Social Welfare—a covert intelligence-gathering unit that would spearhead Tibetan resistance.

At first, the Chinese hid Gyalo Thondup's flight from the Dalai Lama, and suspected him of involvement in the escape. They were disappointed in their treatment by the Tibetans, and now suspected that the Dalai Lama had not only helped Thubten Jigme Norbu flee after betraying them but also helped Gyalo Thondup elude their control. A major blow to their plans, they realized they had failed to win the Dalai Lama over.

THE DALAI LAMA TRAVELS TO CHINA

In hopes of increasing favor with the Dalai Lama, the Chinese government issued an invitation, asking that he lead a Tibetan delegation to the First National People's Congress of the People's Republic of China in Beijing in 1953. Knowing his taste for modernity, especially heavy industry, they decided to try to impress the Dalai Lama with the power of China. They speculated that once he saw the progress there, he would be anxious to have the same reforms for his own people.

Although the Dalai Lama was wise enough to see that the Chinese intended to use his presence in Beijing as proof that Tibet had become part of China, he thought that if he could go there and speak with the central government, he might be able to explain the Tibetan people to them. He wanted to make clear which reforms were suitable for them and which were not. By doing so, he hoped to change the course of action of the Chinese administrators in Lhasa.

Yet when his people heard of the trip, they were terrified that he would leave and never come back. Gyalo Thondup sent pleas from India that he not go to China and delegations came from all over the country, begging the Dalai Lama to change his mind. Although the Dalai Lama assured everyone that he was going of his own free will and promised to return, the people did not believe him. They were sure he was traveling on orders from the Chinese.

In the summer of 1954, a party of close to five hundred set out for China, including the Dalai Lama; his mother; his sister Tsering Dolma; his brothers Lobsang Samten and Tendzin Choegyal; two tutors; and other Tibetan officials, along with their servants. A formal departure was set on the bank of the Kyichu River, which included musical bands and followers numbering in the tens of thousands, carrying banners and burning incense to wish the Dalai Lama a safe, successful journey.

The travelers crossed the river in yak-skin boats, on the first leg of a difficult two-thousand-mile journey. What made it most difficult was that no roads connected the two countries, though the Chinese had already begun working on the Qinghai Highway, using forced Tibetan labor. Although the road was not complete, the Dalai Lama was able to travel the first ninety miles of the journey in the Thirteenth Dalai Lama's Dodge, which had also been brought across the river. His first stop was at Ganden Monastery.

After spending a few days resting and praying, he continued on, but soon had to exchange his automobile for a mule at the Kongpo region, where the road had been washed out. The travelers then faced the dangers of flash flooding and landslides, as huge boulders crashed down to meet the party. Owing to the summer season and heavy rains, long stretches of the trail were covered in mud, eighteen or more inches deep. Although the Tibetans urged the Chinese to take higher roads rather than follow the projected route of the road under construction, the Chinese ignored them. Three young soldiers, employed in protecting the Dalai Lama and his party from the landslides, died along the way—as did many mules and horses—when boulders fell on them or they tumbled over the edge of cliffs.

When the party finally reached Chamdo, a large reception met the Dalai Lama and his party. As the capital of Kham was administered solely by Chinese at the time, martial music was played for the glory of Chairman Mao and the revolution and local Tibetans stood waving red flags. This was disconcerting for the Lhasans in the traveling party, as it was their first experience in a wholly Chinese Communist Tibet.

At Chengdu, just across the Chinese border, the Dalai Lama proceeded by Jeep. However, he fell ill with fever and was confined to bed for several days. After his health was restored, he met with the Panchen Lama who had traveled to Shigang from his home in Shigatse, as he had been invited to tour China along with the Dalai Lama. The Panchen Lama figured high in China's bid to absorb Tibet, as the Panchen Lama had been under Chinese control for many years.

In 1910, before the fall of the Qing dynasty, when China invaded Tibet and the Thirteenth Dalai Lama had gone into exile in India, the previous Panchen Lama's supporters had taken the opportunity to criticize the Thirteenth Dalai Lama's administration of the government. The Chinese used this dissension as a way to widen the gap between the first and second rulers of Tibet, and when the Chinese were driven from the country in 1911, the Ninth Panchen Lama moved into Chinese territory, where he lived for the rest of his life.

When the reincarnation of the Panchen Lama was found, in 1944, he was enthroned at Kumbum Monastery, but he was not recognized by the Tibetan government as the true Panchen Lama until 1951 because he had been "found" by the Chinese. He had not been tested, as was the Dalai Lama, but to avoid acrimony with the Chinese, the Tibetan government agreed to allow the office to be chosen by lottery divination. Conveniently, the same candidate was chosen, the Chinese were appeased, and the new Panchen Lama was formally accepted by all of Tibet. All of the Tenth Panchen Lama's training had been accomplished under the eye of the Chinese, and they had recently stepped up efforts to use him in gathering Tibetans to their cause.

The high lamas had met before, in Lhasa, when the Panchen Lama was recognized and presented to the Dalai Lama in a formal ceremony when he was fourteen. At the time of the China tour, he was just sixteen, and the Dalai Lama nineteen. Together they and their party were flown to Xian, and the last leg of the journey was completed by train.

AN IMPRESSIVE AND CONFUSING STAY

Zhou En-lai, the Chinese prime minister, greeted the Dalai and Panchen Lamas as they got off the train. The Dalai Lama was then taken to a bungalow with a beautiful garden, which had once been the home of the Japanese diplomatic mission. A Tibetan who had been converted to Communism before the takeover in Tibet would be the Dalai Lama's interpreter for the length of his stay.

Just a few days after his arrival, the Dalai Lama was invited to a banquet to meet Chairman Mao. A cult of personality had formed around the chairman in China. Many Chinese, especially students in his Red Guard, worshipped Mao as a deity, and his image was everywhere. His followers dressed like him; chanted "May Mao Zedong live for a thousand years";

and waved copies of his "Little Red Book" (*Quotations from Chairman Mao*), filled with Mao's insights, including the famous "Political power grows out of the barrel of a gun."[11]

The Dalai Lama was not intimidated by Mao's popularity but said of him, "I felt as if I was in the presence of a strong magnetic force."[12] The two leaders seemed to get along well and had several meetings while the Dalai Lama was in Beijing.

Tibet and its future was the topic of conversation. Because the Dalai Lama was convinced that Tibetans could not oust the Chinese, he was determined to try to make the arrangement bearable. Mao told him that China was presently helping Tibet, but that in twenty years, the table might be turned, and Tibet would help China. The Dalai Lama respected Mao as a great leader and even accepted a position as the vice president of the Steering Committee of the People's Republic of China. The Dalai Lama realized that it was a nominal appointment but, nonetheless, very prestigious and a token of goodwill.

The Dalai Lama also met the prime minister of India, Jawaharlal Nehru, while in Beijing. He had looked forward to the meeting, hoping to discuss the Tibetan situation with the Indian leader. Yet the meeting was formal and there was no opportunity for discussion, which sorely disappointed the Tibetan ruler.

In the winter of 1954, the Dalai Lama went on an extensive tour of China. The country's heavy industry, such as mining, steel, iron, and especially the hydroelectric plant, impressed him, and he became eager for Tibet to make the same progress. Yet the tour was orchestrated by the Chinese to show only sites that would have this effect. The Chinese did not allow the Tibetans to see the poor people of China, who were forced to live in communes, to sublimate their individuality, and to work in state factories or on collective farms.

The Dalai Lama arrived back in Beijing in time to celebrate Losar, the Tibetan New Year, in 1955. To mark the occasion, he hosted a banquet and invited the four most important men in China at that time—Chairman Mao; Prime Minister Zhou En-lai; Liu Shaoqi, Mao's anticipated successor; and Zhu De, commander of the Communist forces. They all accepted. At one point, the Dalai Lama threw a pinch of tsampa into the air, which is a Tibetan expression of good wishes for all. Chairman Mao took a pinch and threw it on the floor. The Dalai Lama ignored the slight, as he did not want to ruin the party, but he began to feel more suspicious of Mao's previously conciliatory behavior.

A few days later, at their last meeting, Mao told the Dalai Lama, "I understand you very well. But of course, religion is poison. It has two great defects: It undermines the race, and secondly, it retards the progress of the country. Tibet and Mongolia have both been poisoned by it."[13] This remark stunned the Dalai Lama. While he had leaned toward forming a positive opinion of the man, and considered accepting his Marxist philosophies as beneficial to his people, he suddenly realized that Mao was the enemy of Buddhism, and that deeper trouble for Tibet was on the way.

NOTES

1. Quoted in Tsering Shakya, *The Dragon in the Land of Snows*, pp. 81–82.
2. Tenzin Gyatso, *Freedom in Exile*, p. 66.
3. The Dalai Lama of Tibet, *My Land and My People*, p. 68.
4. Quoted in Roger Hicks and Ngakpa Chogyam, *Great Ocean*, p. 83.
5. Quoted in Tsering Shakya, *The Dragon in the Land of Snows*, p. 90.
6. Avedon, *In Exile in the Land of Snows*, p. 37.
7. Quoted in Tsering Shakya, *The Dragon in the Land of Snows*, pp. 107–108.
8. Quoted in the Dalai Lama of Tibet, *My Land and My People*, p. 72.
9. Ibid., p. 75.
10. Quoted in Mary Craig, *Kundun*, p. 169.
11. Quoted in "Mao: Model Answer," the History Channel, www.thehistory channel.co.uk/classroom/alevel/mao.htm.
12. Tenzin Gyatso, *Freedom in Exile*, p. 88.
13. Quoted in the Dalai Lama of Tibet, *My Land and My People*, p. 88.

The Fourteenth Dalai Lama as a child, ca. 1935.
© Hulton-Deutsch Collection/CORBIS

The Dalai Lama, age 16, being taught by Lord
Chamberlain of Tibet, 1951.
© Bettman/CORBIS

The Dalai Lama, with unnamed attendants, arriving in India after his exile from Tibet, April 18, 1959. AP Photo

The Dalai Lama accepting the Nobel Peace Prize in Norway, December 10, 1989. AP Photo/Inge Gjellesvik

Chapter 7

BREAKDOWN AND FAILURE
OF RELATIONS

The Dalai Lama arrived back in Lhasa on June 29, 1955. His travel to and from China, his meetings with Chinese officials, and his tour of China had lasted almost one year, and much of what he knew of Lhasa had changed. The road from Xining, on which he had made part of his trip to China, had been opened, and another from Chengdu, in the east, had been opened the previous December. The Chengdu road was the highest road in the world at that time—thirteen thousand feet in altitude—and it stretched from Chengdu in the Szechwan province of China to Lhasa, a total of 1,413 miles. Not only passenger-type vehicles but military trucks now traversed the city streets with traffic so heavy that a uniformed traffic director had to be installed to keep order. Traffic noise and pollution reigned in the once-quiet capital.

Although Lhasans had begun to install electricity before the Chinese invasion, the lines had now been extended and a telephone system put into service, along with telegraph routes to Shigatse, Yadong, and Gyantse. A bridge had been built over the Kyichu River, making it no longer necessary to cross by boat, as the Dalai Lama had done the year before.

The architecture of Lhasa had also changed. A new district had arisen, including a hospital, a movie theater, a bank, a newspaper, and a secondary school. Although it was built primarily to accommodate Communist officials and their families, many Tibetans were impressed. "I had to admit that I was impressed by the fact that they were doing things that would directly benefit the common people," said one Tibetan educator. "It was more change for the good in a shorter period of time than I had seen in my life— more change, I was tempted to think, than Tibet had seen in centuries."[1]

Tibetan traditionalists, however, worried that the new "enhancements" would overwhelm the capital city and that Lhasa, as Tibetans knew it, would be no more. One worry they had not considered was that their economy was being cycled back to China. The Lhasan branch of the State Bank of China made interest-free loans for Tibetan traders and business-men, encouraging them to carry Chinese goods. After the roads were completed, the Lhasan market was flooded with merchandise from China. Tibetans spent their money on these items and, in turn, many silver coins went right back to China.

Although the famine had eased, common Tibetans were still uneasy and resentful of the Chinese intervention in Lhasa. Due to the continued unrest of the people, Chinese soldiers dug trenches around their quarters and laid sandbags around them. No longer did they go out alone or in pairs, but traveled in whole convoys to preserve their safety.

Though Lhasa had begun to take on a new face, the Dalai Lama re-mained optimistic, and wanted to pursue the new order in a spirit of com-promise. He thought that Mao had given him a vote of confidence during his trip to China, and though he was wary of some of his actions, he still saw Mao as a great leader.

Rumors of Chinese atrocities to the Tibetan people in the eastern eth-nic regions had already met the ears of many Lhasans, however, and the Dalai Lama had heard some stories of mistreatment on his way back from China. Accounts ranged from public beatings of Tibetan lamas to public executions, performed by the Tibetans' own children. It was said that the Communists regularly pulled ordinary citizens from their homes, tied them up, and publicly humiliated them by spitting on them, kicking them and ordering them to admit "crimes against the people"—at gunpoint—in what the Communists referred to as struggle sessions. But due to the lack of communication between Tibetan provinces, the stories were still only stories. As the people of Lhasa saw only Chinese improvements in there city, they found the stories difficult to believe, and many saw them as rampant gossip.

OUTCRY IN THE EAST

Toward the end of 1954, Tibetans of the eastern provinces had already begun to vent their rage. Collective farming run by the Chinese proved fruitless, as they were unaccustomed to growing crops in Tibetan soil at such high altitudes. They planted wheat instead of barley—the basis for tsampa. Production did nothing to alleviate the food shortages, as the

Tibetans had little use for wheat. Furthermore, the harvest was poor, and the Chinese exacted taxes from it.

People in the outlying regions were discontented, but the Chinese made a crucial mistake in further antagonizing the men of Kham. The people of Kham are referred to as Khampas, and the men were often seen with Khampa knives hanging from their belts and rifles proudly hung over the fireplaces in their homes. Knowing their fierce natures, the Chinese worried about the widespread availability of weapons in Kham. They offered the Khampas a period of amnesty, time to relinquish their weapons without repercussion, which the Khampas overwhelmingly ignored. Subsequently, the Chinese went about confiscating Khampa guns.

Khampa warriors, angered by this action, assembled by the thousands. They rode through People's Liberation Army (PLA) camps, executing soldiers and forcing the survivors to retreat.

This action brought inevitable retaliation from the Communists. In February, the Chinese bombed Changtreng Sampheling Monastery, where three thousand monks and thousands of villagers had taken refuge. Still, after six months of fighting, the Chinese had suffered terrible losses east of the Yangtze River.

Meanwhile, the commander of the PLA in Chamdo summoned the Chamdo Liberation Committee, composed of 350 prominent Khampa citizens, to the city and asked them to endorse Communist "democratic reforms." The program—begun in early 1955 throughout China and extended to Tibet—would establish several thousand agricultural cooperatives in its eastern regions. The Dalai Lama and his cabinet had already agreed to the reforms; however, the majority vote in Chamdo was a resounding no from the Chamdo Liberation Committee. Attempting to get the vote they desired, the Chinese held the same type of meeting four times, and each time, the vote was the same.

Finally, a fifth meeting was held at the fortress of Jomdho Dzong, forty miles to the northeast of Chamdo, with 210 Kham leaders in attendance. When all of the delegates were inside, 5,000 Chinese troops surrounded the fort and made the Kham leaders prisoners, telling them that the reforms would take place immediately. For two weeks, the Khampas continued to offer resistance. Finally, after much intimidation, they agreed to assent, hoping the Chinese would relax security.

The plan worked, and on the sixteenth day, all 210 men escaped into the Himalayas. Having turned most of the Khampa leadership into outlaws, the Chinese inadvertently initiated the Khampa guerilla movement.

THE PREPARATORY COMMITTEE FOR THE AUTONOMOUS REGION OF TIBET

Before the fighting began, while the Dalai Lama was in China, the Preparatory Committee for the Autonomous Region of Tibet (PCART) was established as a way for Tibet's administration and that of the Chinese Communists in Lhasa to mingle. It was also an assuagement to Tibet, allowing them to feel that they were regaining control of Lhasan politics after China's mismanagement of the capital.

The Dalai Lama welcomed the formation of this body. He saw it as a way to reach agreement through a shared administration. He advocated a system of compromise, in which the needs of his people could be met and, perhaps, improved by the Chinese. For many years, he had been interested in bringing Tibet into the twentieth century and saw China as the vehicle by which the renaissance might be achieved.

PCART's constitution created new departments in the Tibetan government to oversee finance, agriculture, education, medicine, religion, and security, and all were to be run by citizens of Tibet. The administration of Chamdo was to return to Lhasa, while the rest of Kham and Amdo would remain under direct Chinese control. Of fifty-one regional delegates, including the Dalai Lama, only five were to be Chinese; the cabinet and the National Assembly would remain in power.

What seemed reasonable in theory became less appealing in practice. The Chinese handed out the forty-five Tibetan posts to those who wished to keep their property and power in exchange for compliance. The PCART creation also gave the Panchen Lama the same status and power in the Shigatse region as the Dalai Lama had in Lhasa, made him vice chairman of the PCART, and allowed him to select his own representatives to the committee. Lhasan officials were not pleased, and although the Dalai Lama was slated as chairman of PCART, he could do nothing about the situation. This made the circumstances tenuous, owing to the Panchen Lama's Chinese influences. It was clear that Lhasa and Shigatse would find it difficult to cooperate. Ngabo Ngawang Jigme, now in open collaboration with the Chinese, was also installed as PCART's secretary-general. This meant that non-Communist supporters made up only 27 percent of the governing body. The cabinet and the National Assembly were outvoted two to one on every issue, and the Dalai Lama soon realized that he had been made head of the committee in order to appease his people.

Nonetheless, the inauguration of the PCART was held on April 22, 1956, in Tibet's first auditorium—the Lhasa Hall—which sat directly opposite the Potala. During his speech to the assembly, the Dalai Lama urged Chinese leaders to be more cautious when adopting reforms, especially in the eastern territories of Kham and Amdo.

Shortly after the inauguration, Lobsang Samten was appointed to the newly created Security Department, which amused the Dalai Lama, knowing his brother to be gentle and passive. Lobsang Samten also found the appointment ludicrous, and that evening, he asked the Dalai Lama how he should react. As a member of the Dalai Lama's family, he could not flatly turn the appointment down, lest he bring added pain for his brother.

The Dalai Lama's oldest brother, Thubten Jigme Norbu, was in Calcutta during this time with his other brother Gyalo Thondup and his sister Tsering Dolma. She had been with the Dalai Lama's traveling party in China the previous year, and for the same reason that Lobsang Samten accepted his appointment to the Security Department, she pleaded with her younger brothers to return to Lhasa. Thubten Jigme Norbu wrote, "[Tsering Dolma] had been told that she must do her utmost to get the fugitive members of the Dalai Lama's family to return to Tibet .... She was afraid that our obstinate refusal to go back would cause the Dalai Lama still further difficulties."[2]

These anxieties would have been normal for any family, but as Tibetan Buddhists, the Dalai Lama's siblings also revered him as a god. They would need great strength and courage to disregard that fact and remain in exile, without regard for his well-being. Alternatively, returning to Tibet might mean enslavement, punishment, or even death at the hands of the Communists for all of them. Both Thubten Jigme Norbu and Gyalo Thondup told their sister that as long as the Communists were in Tibet, there was no going back. They decided that either choice might have dire consequences for the Dalai Lama. Tsering Dolma returned to Lhasa and blamed her inability to repatriate her brothers on their innate stubbornness.

Nothing had improved in her absence. The PCART was a sham; central Tibet was under the control of the Committee of the Chinese Communist Party in Tibet, which had no Tibetan members. When the people realized this, unrest intensified. New resistance groups sprang up. Their leaders voiced their opinions of PCART, saying that Tibet had its own system of administration and that PCART was unnecessary and should be abolished. The Communists hurried to suppress the demonstrations and drafted a new proclamation to ban public meetings. The Dalai Lama was forced to sign the regulation, knowing that banning public meetings would never alter public opinion.

He admired the people involved in resisting the Chinese and was proud that such leadership and will was Tibetan, yet he was totally committed to his Buddhist teachings. He maintained compassion for the Chinese and eschewed all violence. Knowing the people were stirring to revolt, he considered resigning as Dalai Lama to appease the Chinese, and allowing them to take complete control in order to keep his people safe. In the end, he retained his position but knew he had to condemn the uprisings. If he advocated violence, it might mean machine gunning in the streets and bombing of national treasures. The Dalai Lama opted instead to buy time, hoping for outside intervention, while lulling the Chinese into a false sense of security through his cooperation.

While the public remained loyal to the Dalai Lama, by virtue of his god-king status, they were not so eager to accept cabinet decisions. They blamed the cabinet for weakness; the cabinet opted to keep resisters from violent repercussions.

Battles continued to rage in the eastern provinces. In February 1956, a militia formed to defend Lithang Monastery, and in answer, the PLA drafted forty thousand more troops. Fighting at the monastery lasted for sixty-four days before it was bombed on June 1, killing 800 monks and many lay citizens.

After the shelling stopped, survivors were tortured and killed. Monks and nuns were forced to break their vows of celibacy by having sexual intercourse with one another in public, at gunpoint. The Dalai Lama heard the news and he cried. He asked the Chinese, "How are Tibetans supposed to trust the Chinese if this is how you behave?"[3] The Chinese saw the Dalai Lama's criticisms as insults to the motherland. They told him that if the Tibetans could not see that the reforms would be good for them, they needed to be punished.

The Dalai Lama sent a letter to Mao immediately, asking him to intervene, hoping he would see that his emissaries were not following his instructions. There was no reply. The Dalai Lama sent a second and a third letter, to which no answers came. He accepted the fact that the soldiers carrying out the atrocities on the Tibetan people were following the path Mao had drawn for them.

Refugees from the outer regions had begun migrating to Lhasa in 1954. By 1956, the numbers of such refugees had begun to overwhelm the city. One of them said, "Perhaps for the first time in its history, Lhasa became a goal, a focal point, not for pilgrims but for men of war."[4] Perhaps twenty thousand were en route when Chinese planes began to strafe and bombard them. Both animals and marchers died from exhaustion and exposure, and many simply fell from the steep cliffs, where they traveled to protect themselves from the onslaught. They had only one hope for their people in the east—the Dalai Lama.

A WELCOME INVITATION

In 1956, the president of the Maha Bodhi Society, an organization dedicated to Buddhist spiritual and educational development, brought the Dalai Lama an invitation. He was welcomed to attend the Buddha Jayanti celebrations, in honor of the 2,500th anniversary of the Buddha's birth, which was to be celebrated throughout India. This brightened his spirits, and he hoped to be able to attend.

To all Tibetans, India is the holy land—the birthplace of Buddhism—and the Dalai Lama had always wanted to visit. While in India, he also hoped to see the burial place and heirs of Mahatma Gandhi, the Indian spiritual leader, who forced Great Britain to grant independence to India through his practice of nonviolent disobedience. The Dalai Lama greatly admired him, but also hoped to meet Prime Minister Nehru again. His intention was to ask for Nehru's guidance and assistance. He was also anxious to see how democracy worked in India—for a respite from the Communist struggle—and to renew his contacts with the British embassy in India. He saw Great Britain as Tibet's only true lifeline to foreign politics in the world, but since Indian independence, the countries' association had faded away.

Knowing that he could not leave Tibet without Chinese assent, the Dalai Lama took the invitation to the senior Chinese general, who offered "suggestions" why the Dalai Lama should not attend, citing security reasons. He also told him the PCART still had much work to do, and that the Dalai Lama was integral in those projects. The general said that since the invitation had come from a religious organization rather than the Indian government, there was no need to accept it, and advised him to send a representative. The Dalai Lama was devastated but knew that arguing would do no good. The Chinese would never allow him to go, so he tried to put the idea from his mind.

On October 1, Prime Minister Nehru sent a telegram to Peking, asking that both the Dalai Lama and the Panchen Lama be permitted to attend the Buddha Jayanti. The Chinese relented, owing to the official government invitation, as they did not want their refusal to injure Sino-Indian relations. Zhang Jinwu told the Dalai Lama that he could go, and would be protected by the Chinese ambassador to India. He spoke to the Dalai Lama about the people's uprising in Hungary and Poland and reminded him of how they had suffered at the hands of the Russians, who put down the reactionaries, and said that the Communist bloc was strong and would help its allies. This allusion was to China's potential enlistment of outside help in the Tibetan struggle. The Dalai Lama knew he meant that if he involved Russia, his people would suffer more intensely than they had already suffered, as Russia's history of dealing with dissidents, under the leadership of Joseph Stalin, had been far rougher than China's, and their military might was far stronger.

The Dalai Lama's speeches for the trip had to be written beforehand and approved by the Chinese. Any questions about the situation in Tibet were to be answered by him with either an assurance that although there were slight "disturbances," all was well, or an assertion that the question was a matter for Beijing. He was also to refuse to take part in the celebration if any representatives from Taiwan were present, as Jiang Jie-shi's nationalists had retreated to the island and set up an independent government there, and the two factions were still involved in a cold war. The Chinese ambassador was to give the Dalai Lama the latest information on the Jayanti's guest list upon his arrival in India.

In mid-November, the Dalai Lama and his party left Lhasa. Thanks to the new Chinese road system, much of the journey could be completed by automobile. They stopped at Shigatse to pick up the Panchen Lama, then proceeded on to the last Tibetan settlement before the border, where, to the Dalai Lama's delight, they parted with their Chinese escort. For the first time in years, he was free to move about without supervision. At Yadong, they exchanged their wheels for horses.

Just over the Nathu La Pass at the border of Sikkim, the party was greeted by an honor guard, a band, and a small group of dignitaries. Beside frozen Lake Tsongo, they would spend the night in a camp of tents. When the Dalai Lama arrived, he was thrilled to see Thubten Jigme Norbu and Gyalo Thondup there to greet him. He had seen neither brother for several years. Since Lobsang Samten and Tendzin Choegyal had accompanied the Dalai Lama from Lhasa, the five brothers were together for the first time ever. "It was a solemn moment, but then once again the questions and answers started up on all sides, for there was a tremendous amount to tell," wrote Thubten Jigme Norbu. "At the wish of the Dalai Lama we were spending the whole evening together."[5]

During that time, Thubten Jigme Norbu told the Dalai Lama that outsiders had begun to show interest in the plight of Tibet, and that help might be on the way. He did not come right out and tell him, however, that Gyalo Thondup had already been in contact with the American CIA.

The next morning, the brothers separated again. All but the Dalai Lama would travel to New Delhi via Calcutta, where they would meet the other members of the family—their mother, Tsering Dolma, and Jetsun Pema. The Dalai Lama was taken to Gangtok, where he spent the night, and the next day to Bagdogra Airfield, just inside the Indian border. He was flown to New Delhi, where he was met, with great fanfare, by Prime Minister Jawaharlal Nehru and many from India's diplomatic corps.

The following day, his first visit was to Rajghat on the banks of the Jamuna River, where the great Mahatma Gandhi had been cremated. The Dalai Lama regretted never meeting the great leader in person, but felt great joy over the example he had set for millions during his lifetime. He most admired his adoption of the doctrine of ahimsa—the pursuit of nonviolence.

THE HIGH LAMA SPEAKS OUT
AND IS DISAPPOINTED

For the next few days, the Dalai Lama was busy with celebrating the Buddha Jayanti. He took the opportunity to talk to followers and family members of Gandhi, and spoke at a meeting of the United Nations Educational, Scientific, and Cultural Organization (UNESCO) in New Delhi. The Dalai Lama threw his prepared speeches away and spoke to the crowd, carefully. He told them that while the entire world preached peace, large nations were usurping smaller ones. He admonished them not to allow the injustices to pass unnoticed.

When the celebrations ended, the Dalai Lama had his first meeting with Prime Minister Nehru. The Dalai Lama told the Indian leader that he was considering staying in India and asked if he would be offered asylum. Nehru balked. He told the Dalai Lama that peace in Asia depended on good relations between India and China.

Through its signing and ratification of the Seventeen-Point Agreement, Tibet had become part of China de facto, and—in India's eyes— had relinquished its rights to international discussions. In 1954, the Indian government had signed a trade agreement with the Chinese, whereby they agreed to withdraw their military escorts, stationed at Yadong and Gyantse, and to transfer, without charge, the telegraph and telephone installations in Tibet that were operated by India. The wording of the treaty unequivocally accepted China's sovereignty over Tibet, where historically they had only thought of China as Tibet's suzerain.

Nehru told the Dalai Lama that as much as he sympathized with him, he could not endanger the peace of the region. Nehru urged him to return to Lhasa and to work with the Chinese, under the terms of the Seventeen-Point Agreement. Although the Dalai Lama protested that he had done that for the past seven years, Nehru flatly told him that India could not support him. He did, however, promise to speak to the Chinese prime minister, Zhou En-lai, who was to arrive in Delhi the following day.

The Dalai Lama visited the airport with Nehru the following morning, and a meeting was set with Zhou En-lai that night. Zhou said that it was rumored that the Dalai Lama planned to stay in India. In blunt terms, Zhou told the Dalai Lama that it would be a huge mistake, as his country needed him.

Thubten Jigme Norbu and Gyalo Thondup also met with Zhou En-lai in New Delhi. He subtly directed them to return to Tibet, but they flatly refused. They recounted all they had seen and heard and what others had told them of the events taking place in Tibet. Zhou En-lai advised them that it was the wish of the People's Republic of China to improve conditions in Tibet and to allow the people to share in its progress. Zhou also said that the Dalai Lama had an integral part to play in their plans and that his speedy return to Lhasa was vital.

After those meetings, the Dalai Lama, his family, and the Panchen Lama, boarded a train—which had been placed at the Tibetan delegation's disposal—and traveled to various Buddhist shrines, including Sanchi, Ajanta, Benares, Bodh Gaya, and other sites around the country. The Dalai Lama's sister Jetsun Pema wrote of the journey:

> It was during this journey across India that I really got to know The Dalai Lama. I was then sixteen and he was twenty-one. We visited the aircraft factory in Bangalore and the site of the hydroelectric plant in Nangal. He was fascinated and did not miss any opportunity to compare his journey to China in 1954 with his impressions of India. He talked a lot about the differences between Communism and a young democracy in which liberty soared.[6]

The Dalai Lama returned to New Delhi after three months of traveling. Zhou En-lai had returned, as well, and met with the Dalai Lama again. Zhou admitted that the situation in Tibet was getting out of hand and that the Chinese would use greater force, if necessary, to control the disturbances. The Dalai Lama took his stern declarations as intimidation, and knew then that he had no choice but to return to his homeland.

He spent a few days with his family, and during that time, his brothers tried to convince him not to return. The Dalai Lama said that he could not remain in safety while his people were left at the mercy of the Chinese. However, due to blizzards in the Himalayas, he was stuck in India for another month.

Parting with his brother and most trusted companion, Lobsang Samten, who had decided to stay in India, was difficult for the Dalai Lama. Diki Tsering also wished for her son Tendzin Choegyal to stay, but the older sons were against it. He, too, had been declared an incarnate lama, and the brothers said it was his place to stay in Tibet for as long as possible. Diki Tsering would also return, though not right away.

COVERT OPERATIONS

What the Dalai Lama did not know was that his brothers had been working with the CIA. Referring to Gyalo Thondup, Jetsun Pema described his involvement: "My brother recruited young Tibetans who were sent to Arizona to be trained by the CIA. They then returned and were parachuted in small groups over certain regions of Tibet. Very few people knew about this at the time, and no one talked about it. Some of the people were captured and tortured, others had a cyanide pill to prevent them from falling alive into the hands of the Chinese."[7]

Gyalo Thondup had formed the Committee for Tibetan Social Welfare in Darjeeling, India, in 1954, and rebels had been in contact with him, asking for weapons and training. Through the nationalists in Taiwan, he had arms and supplies dropped over Tibet. Then, through Thubten Jigme Norbu, who brought the news to India, Gyalo Thondup was offered American support.

The United States, however, did not want to become openly involved in Tibet. Due to Tibet's ratification of the Seventeen-Point Agreement and the Dalai Lama's participation in PCART and the Chinese National People's Congress while he was in China, the Americans believed that the Tibetan government had willingly ended Tibet's independence. They agreed to take a more active part in the Tibetan situation, but only if they were asked to do so by the Tibetan government.

The Americans were not specifically interested in helping Tibet as much as they were interested in stopping the spread of Communism. In 1955, U.S. President Dwight D. Eisenhower authorized the CIA to develop groups to destabilize the country; however, the CIA plot failed. The Khampas, who were chosen for the program, trained for one year and then parachuted back into Tibet to organize and train guerrilla groups in different areas of the country. But the United States would not contribute any weapons that could be traced back to them—only old bazookas and British rifles that were also dropped from airplanes, many of them breaking on impact from the fall. Meanwhile, the PLA savagely shelled villages throughout the region, and their numbers grew to 150,000 troops. The Tibetan troops were simply overwhelmed.

However, nothing could impede Tibetan fervor. Other guerrilla organizations rose up in hopes of regaining the country. By the time the Dalai Lama had returned to Lhasa on April 1, the city was in suspension and turmoil at the same time. Zhou En-lai had ordered some superficial changes, such as decreasing the number of troops and removing some political officers associated with some unpopular reforms. Work was also halted on a new army barracks and a controversial hydroelectric plant. Although the Chinese did not intend to change their policies, they wanted Tibetans to think they had backed off. They had, in fact, agreed to postpone any further reforms for six years. Fighting was intensifying in the provinces, and they hoped to maintain order in the Tibetan capital at least.

However, Lhasa was inundated with refugees, and held more than ten thousand tents, mainly for Khampas. Most Lhasans considered Khampas bandits, and were intimidated by their presence. The Khampas also brought stories of atrocities perpetrated on Tibetans in their homeland. The combination of hatred for the Chinese and the increasing competition for space and resources made the Lhasans furious.

The Dalai Lama saw that the situation throughout Tibet had deteriorated considerably in five months. Open warfare was taking place all over the provinces of Kham and Amdo. Towns and villages were being devastated by bombs and artillery barrage. Tibet was in chaos.

As a gesture toward loyalty and unity, a Khampa businessman, Gompo Tashi Andrugtsang, had undertaken a project to have an exquisite throne made for the Dalai Lama, shortly before the end of 1956. He went about soliciting donations, and under the guise of this patriotic and deferential pursuit, he also sought to enlist guerrilla fighters. They organized themselves under the traditional name for the combined outer regions—Four Rivers, Six Ranges.

During the middle of 1958, neither the Chinese nor the Tibetans had much control over the course of events in Tibet. Although the Dalai Lama admired the Khampa warriors and appreciated their zeal to wrest Tibet from the grip of the Chinese, he could not stand behind them. He tried to preserve some semblance of order in the capital, and to stand by his policy of passive resistance.

A SEMBLANCE OF NORMAL LIFE

In the face of so much turmoil, the Dalai Lama went about preparing for the hardest examination of his life—a doctorate in metaphysics, the Geshe degree, which is the highest academic degree awarded in Tibet. The examinations involved intensive debating on a wide range of subjects against the wisest minds in Tibet. Although the course usually took a man twenty years to complete, the Dalai Lama took only half the time. He set the date of the exam for the Great Prayer Festival in 1959, which would occur in late February to early March. The Dalai Lama felt pressured to pass the examination, as his time might be running out. There was no guarantee that the Chinese would permit him to take such an examination in the future or that he would even be alive. He needed proper time to prepare his mind.

To allow him some respite, in the spring of 1958, the Dalai Lama assumed new living quarters at the Norbulingka. As it was tradition for each Dalai Lama to erect his own building within the Norbulingka, he had a small house constructed. The most exciting feature for him was that the "palace" was fitted with modern appliances. He had an iron bed, as opposed to his traditional platform bed, and a bathroom, complete with running water and plumbing. The two-story house also had electricity; chairs and tables, rather than Tibetan cushions; and a radio, which he had received from the Indian government. Outside, he had a small pond and a garden, where he could personally supervise planting. He was very happy in his new home, though only for a short time.

The Dalai Lama's personal trouble with Chinese officials worsened. Later in that year, Four Rivers, Six Ranges attacked a three thousand-man PLA garrison at Tsethang, about thirty miles outside of Lhasa, and overran the soldiers. The political commissar demanded that the Dalai Lama mobilize the Tibetan army against his own people. When the Dalai Lama pointed out that if he did so, the army would most likely desert to join the freedom fighters, the commissar became very angry. He screamed that all Tibetans were ungrateful, warning that this resistance would end badly for them. He identified several Tibetans in exile, including Thubten Jigme Norbu and Gyalo Thondup, saying they had been instigating trouble, and ordered the Dalai Lama to revoke their Tibetan citizenship. Because the Dalai Lama was still averse to open fighting in Lhasa, he agreed, knowing that his brothers and the others identified would be safe outside Tibet. The commissar also canceled a scheduled visit by Nehru, saying he could not guarantee the prime minister's safety.

No longer did the Chinese treat the Dalai Lama with kid gloves. He did not kowtow to them, influence his people on their behalf, or step down. But the Dalai Lama was not in favor with the resistance fighters, either, who wanted his approval for their actions. Although he understood them, he still could not condone their violence.

All of this weighed heavily on the Dalai Lama as he went to Drepung in the fall of 1958 for the first part of his monastic examination. However, he passed easily. The next segment of the exam would take place at Ganden Monastery. There, he was under greater pressure, as advisors encouraged him to repudiate the Seventeen-Point Agreement and to reinstate his own government. He gave serious thought to their proposal, but came to the same conclusion. A declaration such as they advised would only provoke an all-out Chinese attack. He passed the second part of his exam and returned to Lhasa to study for the final portion and to endure the cold, lonely winter.

Because of continued fighting and intensifying Chinese pressure to stop it, the Dalai Lama found it hard to focus on his studies. He concentrated on Buddha's teaching that one's enemies are one's greatest teachers, and tried to maintain his compassion for the Chinese. After several long, difficult months, 1959 arrived, and the New Year came upon Tibet. Following closely behind it was the Great Prayer Festival, and Tibetans from all over the country flocked to Lhasa for the occasion.

Shortly after the celebration, two junior Chinese officials came to re-extend General Zhang Jinwu's invitation to the Dalai Lama to a performance of a dance troupe from China. He had offered the invitation before, and the Dalai Lama had been able to beg off politely. This time, they expected a firm date when he could attend. The Dalai Lama put them off again, saying that he was studying for the final leg of his examinations and could not possibly set a date until the tests were over. Appeased, the officials went back to inform the general.

The following morning, the Dalai Lama presented himself for his Geshe debates, which were to be held before many thousands of people. Epistemology and logic were the prenoon topics; Buddhist philosophy would be discussed in the afternoon; and all five of his study regimens—perfection of wisdom, the middle view, valid cognition, discipline, and knowledge—would be discussed until seven o'clock in the evening. When the debating was over, a panel of judges unanimously agreed to award the Dalai Lama the title of Geshe, or doctor of metaphysics.

Two days later, the Chinese were at the Dalai Lama's door, again asking for a date on which he could attend the dance troupe's performance. Knowing he could not put them off again, the Dalai Lama agreed to the tenth of March as convenient.

Not long after the date was set, the Dalai Lama's bodyguard was summoned and told that the Chinese wanted to dispense with the normal formalities. No Tibetan soldiers were to accompany the Dalai Lama as was customary; only two unarmed bodyguards would be permitted, and they expected secrecy regarding the entire arrangement. When the Dalai Lama was informed of Chinese plans, he decided that he had no choice but to agree, and resigned himself to adhering to their dubious arrangements.

PROTECTION AT ANY COST

The Dalai Lama's bodyguards were shocked by the request, and rumors spread to the people, with an unbelievable outcome. On the morning of March 10, people poured out of Lhasa and surrounded the Norbulingka, and by 9 A.M., nearly thirty thousand people had assembled by its front gate. They had decided to protect the Dalai Lama from a Chinese abduction.

The Dalai Lama was anxious to defuse the situation. It seemed that anyone who tried to pass the Norbulingka's gates was in danger and under suspicion of collaborating with the Chinese. One known traitor rode by the crowd on his bicycle and fired two shots to warn the crowd back. He was stoned to death, and his body tied to a horse and dragged through the city streets. The people called for the Chinese to leave Tibet, and were determined not to move.

The Dalai Lama's Lord Chamberlain called General Zhang Jinwu to pass along the Dalai Lama's regrets at not being able to attend the dance troupe's performance, saying that the Dalai Lama hoped the crowd would disburse and that order would be quickly restored. The Chinese were outraged and blamed the Tibetan government, which they said had been secretly organizing the demonstration. He also indicated that they could expect necessary force to dispel the uprising.

Of course, the demonstrators must have expected repercussions and did not care. Even the women of the city had massed at the foot of the Potala, daring the Chinese to open fire on them and shouting that Tibet was from that moment a free country.

That evening, seventy government junior officials, the Dalai Lama's personal bodyguard, and several popular leaders, who had gained a modicum of power during Chinese occupation, held a meeting outside the Norbulingka. They signed a declaration, denouncing the Seventeen-Point Agreement, saying they no longer recognized Chinese authority.

Shortly after, the Dalai Lama received a message from the Chinese, suggesting that he move to their headquarters for protection. Of course, doing such a thing was impossible, if not ridiculous, as the Chinese were the very people the demonstrators were trying to protect the Dalai Lama from.

The Dalai Lama went to the Nechung oracle for guidance. Many of his advisors were now advocating his flight, but he was not sure which way to turn. The oracle clearly told him to stay and try to compromise with the Chinese.

On March 16, the Dalai Lama received a letter from the Chinese, again asking him to come to their headquarters. Inside was also a note from Ngabo Ngawang Jigme. This message made it perfectly clear that the Chinese were planning an imminent attack on the people and surrounding the Norbulingka. Ngabo Ngawang Jigme asked for a map of the Norbulingka, indicating where the Dalai Lama would be so that he would not be injured by the shells.

The Dalai Lama replied that he, too, was appalled by the action of the radicals and that he hoped the Chinese would be patient and wait for the crowd to disburse. He knew the crowd could not remain indefinitely and hoped only to buy time for his people, whose lives were in grave danger.

On March 17, at four in the afternoon, the first shots were fired. Two mortar shots destroyed the stillness of the Norbulingka's inner garden. The Dalai Lama quickly consulted the oracle again. This time, the oracle's answer was different. "Go! Go! Tonight!" he shouted, and drew the route the Dalai Lama should take to his exile. The Dalai Lama knew the oracle was right. The only way to protect his people was to leave, so that they would have nothing more to protect. By leaving, he hoped to save thousands of lives.

NOTES

1. Tashi Tsering, Melvyn Goldstein, and William Siebenschuh. *The Struggle for Modern Tibet: The Autobiography of Tashi Tsering* (Armonk, N.Y.: M.E. Sharpe, 1997), p. 41.

2. Thubten Jigme Norbu and Heinrich Harrer. *Tibet Is My Country*, p. 238.

3. Tenzin Gyatso, *Freedom in Exile*, p. 110.

4. Quoted in Noel Barber, *From the Land of Lost Content: The Dalai Lama's Fight for Tibet* (Boston: Houghton Mifflin, 1970), p. 23.

5. Thubten Jigme Norbu and Heinrich Harrer, *Tibet Is My Country*, p. 241.

6. Jetsun Pema, *Tibet: My Story*, p. 54.

7. Ibid., p. 51.

Chapter 8

ESCAPE TO INDIA

As the Dalai Lama agonized over his people gathering outside the Norbulingka, the Chinese were at Drepung Monastery collecting his brother, Tendzin Choegyal, for the dance troupe's performance. Although the boy had looked forward to the entertainment, he recognized turmoil at the Chinese camp the moment he arrived. The commissar was furious that neither the Dalai Lama nor his mother, who had feigned illness, would attend the performance and even more furious at the Tibetan people. He called them "reactionaries" and screamed that he would "liquidate" them if they did not soon obey.

At that moment, Tendzin Choegyal learned of the demonstrations at the Norbulingka; he began to worry for his own safety and freedom and wondered whether the Chinese would hold him hostage in order to control the Dalai Lama. He nervously watched the abbreviated dance performance and was relieved when the driver was ordered to return him to Drepung. However, his mother's servant stopped the car at a crossroads between the camp and her house, which lay behind the first wall of the Norbulingka. The servant lied to the driver and told him that Diki Tsering's illness had worsened. He requested that the boy be returned to her home rather than taken back to the monastery. Tendzin Choegyal jumped from the vehicle and ran the short distance to his mother's house.

Diki Tsering, who was quite well, watched from a window and clapped her hands in delight as she watched her youngest son approaching. She also had feared that the Chinese would take him to China or worse. Diki Tsering, Tsering Dolma, and Tendzin Choegyal spent the night wondering what the following day would bring.

The next day, the commander of the Dalai Lama's bodyguard came to the house and told the family to gather only a few personal items, as the Dalai Lama had decided to flee the country, and warned them not to disclose anything about the escape, even to their closest friends. Diki Tsering was most distraught that she was not able to tell her seventy-year-old mother that she was leaving Tibet, but officials suspected that there were Chinese spies among the servants, and feared discovery of the escape plan.

Tendzin Choegyal shed his maroon monks' robes for a drab soldier's chuba, and under it, strapped on an old Luger (German pistol) he had found in a drawer. To hide his shorn head, he donned a woolen cap. His mother and sister dressed like soldiers, wearing trousers; green fur-lined chubas, such as those worn by Khampa men; maroon hats; and men's boots, which they scrubbed with mud to give them a worn appearance. They would leave at night, to avoid detection.

At nine o'clock on the evening of March 17, the Dalai Lama's family was the first group to go through the gates, including the Dalai Lama's mother, Tsering Dolma, Tendzin Choegyal, his uncle, and a small escort. The former prime minister ordered the gate opened, saying his patrol had been ordered to inspect the riverside. The escape party went right through the crowd, without trouble. "I think I was the misfit because of my height," said Tendzin Choegyal, "but they let us through anyway."[1]

The party crossed an open expanse, dotted with bushes, until they met a man holding a pony for Diki Tsering, who was unable to walk due to her arthritic knee. Then, spread out as a genuine patrol, the family made their way to the river, carrying only meager provisions of tsampa, butter, and meat. Once they made their way to the riverbank, they were transported across the Kyichu River in yak-skin boats, and then waited for the rest of the escape party on the other side.

Inside the inner wall of the Norbulingka, the Dalai Lama prepared his own disguise. He donned a long black overcoat and a pair of trousers, and slipped a rifle over his shoulder. He found it strange to be outside his monk's robes, in a type of clothing he had never worn before.

Before departing, he wrote a letter, certifying the people's leaders, and went to the chapel of the same protective deity that had visited the Dalai Lama's home at his birth as a crow. There he read from the Buddha's teachings, stopping at one about developing confidence and courage. He then took a sacred cloth painting of another protective deity, rolled it, and placed it inside a container to be slung across his back. This painting had belonged to the Second Dalai Lama. His last preparation was to put a fur cap atop his shorn head and to remove his glasses.

The Dalai Lama was terrified but not for himself. If his own people spotted him, they would surely prevent him from leaving. The Dalai Lama was certain that they would be hurt if the demonstrations continued and hoped that, if he left, the crowd would disperse. If he was captured by the Chinese, all hope for Tibet would be lost; since the Dalai Lama is the embodiment of Tibet, his demise would mean the downfall of the entire country and loss of the Tibetan identity.

On the way to his front door, the Dalai Lama stopped to pat one of his dogs. The dog had never been friendly to him, so it was not hard to leave the animal behind. He had more remorse over leaving his old friends—his bodyguards and sweepers. As he left the building, he visualized reaching India and then returning to Tibet, to his position and to the people he loved and had to leave behind.

The Dalai Lama left his residence at ten o'clock and was met by his chief of staff, who was armed with a sword. Among the Dalai Lama's party were the lord chancellor, his chamberlain, the commander of the bodyguard, and two Tibetan soldiers. The chief of staff told the Dalai Lama and his party to stick close by, and as he went through the gate, he announced to the crowd that he was conducting a routine inspection. The people allowed the "soldiers" to pass, without recognizing the Dalai Lama among them.

THE RUGGED TRAIL

This second party made its way to a tributary of the Kyichu River, where it was possible to cross via stepping-stones. Darkness was a major obstacle, but the fact that the Dalai Lama could not see very well without his glasses made the crossing even more perilous. He nearly lost his balance several times, which would have meant not only potential injury but the sound of splashing water and possible discovery. The group was also in danger of being misidentified as Chinese soldiers by Tibetan freedom fighters, who were unaware of the escape, and who might open fire, without question.

When the group reached the banks of the Kyichu, the party boarded other yak-skin boats and crossed the river. Every splash of an oar alarmed them. With so many PLA troops in Lhasa, it was highly unusual that no patrols were out that night. Under low clouds and heavy darkness, the second party made it safely across the water.

About thirty freedom fighters and their leaders met the party on the other side of the river, along with a herd of horses they had quickly gathered from the monasteries. Shortly thereafter, the third party of escapees arrived, consisting of the Dalai Lama's ministers, tutors, and advisors, who had all been smuggled out of Lhasa under a tarpaulin in the back of a truck.

Once they had crossed the Kyichu, the Dalai Lama was able to put on his glasses. He saw the torchlight from the PLA garrison stations only a few hundred yards from where they stood, and the soldiers' closeness unnerved him. He quickly exchanged katas with the resistance leaders, thanked them for preparing his escape, and mounted one of the horses.

Due to the urgency of the situation, the horses and saddles had been gathered hurriedly and fitted out in the dark. The best horses had the worst saddles and were given to lower ranking personnel, while the older mules had the best saddles and were distributed to senior officials. In haste and ignoring protocol, the exiles rode off into the night.

Nothing could be done about the thunder of nearly one hundred horses galloping. However, to the fugitives' favor, the wind blew from the northwest and away from the Chinese camp, carrying the sound away with it. Even so, the first few miles of the journey would be the most perilous, since the Chinese were so near.

For the rest of that night and most of the next day, they rode toward the Brahmaputra River, in Tibetan guerrilla territory. Because there was no road, the horses followed a stony track, alongside the hill above the river. To their right was the Chinese camp, and the party was in danger of river patrols spotting them. Near another island, where Chinese dump trucks traversed day and night carrying quarry stones, illumination from a truck's headlights was a distinct risk, yet no trucks appeared.

The trail itself was hard to follow in the dark. Even the Dalai Lama was lost once and had to turn back to find the right direction. Another time, torches were spotted behind the escapees, which they thought to be the Chinese, close on their trail. But the light came from the torches of guerrilla fighters, guiding wayward members of the huge party back to the proper path. Though the group could not see or hear them, they knew that Khampa guerrillas were in the hills all around, waiting to protect them.

"Before dawn it got so cold that I thought my legs would freeze, but when the sun came up it was crisp and clear, so we all felt a bit refreshed," said Tendzin Choegyal.[2] The party continued on to the base of Sandy Pass, which they reached at about eight in the morning. They stopped to have some tea before riding up the treacherous slope, which peaked above the snow line. "The whole way up [Sandy Pass]," Tendzin Choegyal said, "my fat uncle's saddle kept slipping off and he was desperately clutching his horse's neck. I couldn't stop laughing until we dismounted on the other side, where it's sand, and everyone ran down."[3]

The party continued climbing for four hours until they could navigate the pass. After it, ten miles remained before the Tsangpo River. During this leg of the journey, a terrible sandstorm whipped up. In one respect, the squall was fortunate, as the sand cloud hid the runaways; but, as it filled the riders' eyes, noses, and mouths, it made the ride more treacherous.

Worried that the Chinese might have arrived at the river first, the group plodded through the sandstorm cautiously. The river would be a prime point for the Chinese to intercept the party, as there was only one place to cross and only one ferry. When they reached the landing, the group was relieved to see no soldiers, and forded the river without incident.

BAD NEWS FROM THE EAST

On the far side of the river, they took a short respite at a small village, where inhabitants came out to greet the Dalai Lama. Many of them were crying. In these outer regions, only sparse settlements existed, making this territory suitable for the guerrilla fighters' home. With many more Khampa warriors protecting the escapees from that point onward, it would be difficult for the Chinese to follow unless they had anticipated the escape route and mobilized forces to intercept them. Maintaining strict security, the exiles resumed their journey and continued along until nightfall.

After twenty hours in the saddle, the party finally received its first extended rest at the monastery of Ramé. "The day after I escaped from Lhasa," the Dalai Lama said, "I felt a tremendous sense of relief. Actually the danger was still very much alive."[4] Although the Chinese still hunted him, he realized that he would be able to openly criticize their practices in Tibet from that point on, and experienced a strong surge of freedom.

From the second day onward, traveling seemed more pleasant for the party although the road was just as merciless. Added to their already large 100-person company were now 350 Tibetan soldiers and at least 50 guerrillas. Split into small groups, the people struggled up and down high mountain passes, still covered by winter snow. At one point they encountered a blizzard, which caused the Dalai Lama to worry about his mother and the older members of the party, yet he could do nothing but press on. They traveled by day and rested in villages or monasteries by night.

After meeting with his advisors, the Dalai Lama decided to make Luntze Dzong, close to the Indian border, his destination. At the fort, he planned to repudiate the Seventeen-Point Agreement, reestablish his government, and attempt to open communications with the Chinese. He hoped that the Chinese might see some advantage in compromise and that he could prevent them from shelling Lhasa. However, Luntze Dzong was still days ahead; he hoped he had time to save his people.

The next time the party rested, the Dalai Lama took Tendzin Choegyal into his travel group, hoping that it would help his mother and sister travel faster, which it did. The Dalai Lama was comforted knowing the women were farther away from Lhasa and relatively safer.

At this point, the party was able to tune in to the Voice of America on a small radio receiver they had brought along. The report they heard told only of unrest in Lhasa, adding that the whereabouts of the Dalai Lama were unknown. No news of military action was included.

However, soon after hearing the report, a group of horsemen brought devastating news. Two days after the Dalai Lama's departure, in the early morning hours of March 20, the Chinese had heavily shelled the Norbulingka and set machine guns to the crowd outside it. They also set artillery upon the Potala and the village of Shöl; Jokhang Temple; and the monasteries of Sera, Ganden, and Drepung.

Some of the main buildings in the Norbulingka had been destroyed, and all of the others were damaged to some degree. The Potala suffered damage in the west wing, including damage to the golden mausoleum of the Thirteenth Dalai Lama. The medical college was nearly crushed to the ground. Thousands of Tibetans were on their way to years of incarceration in Chinese prisons, and thousands more bodies lay in the streets, many of them women and children.

In the midst of the carnage, the Chinese searched for the Dalai Lama. Going from corpse to corpse, soldiers examined faces of monks and laity alike, trying to determine his whereabouts. That night, searchers reported the Dalai Lama missing. Subsequent to this discovery, thousands more were killed in bombing.

In the horror of knowing that what he had tried so hard to prevent had actually come to fruition, the Dalai Lama finally understood that negotiations with the Chinese were no longer an option. His respect for the freedom fighters grew. Although he could not condone violence, he at last came to understand why it was necessary; and during this stopover, he had a welcome opportunity to speak with some of the Khampa leaders openly. He told them how much he admired their bravery and that he appreciated their patriotism, and thanked them for helping in his escape. He asked them to understand his proclamations, made while under Chinese control, and his reasons for issuing orders that referred to the Khampas as "reactionaries" and "bandits." At that point, regardless of his Buddhist sentiments, the Dalai Lama could not ask the men to stop fighting for Tibet, as he realized the great sacrifices they had made in leaving their families behind to risk their lives for their country.

One of the leaders told the Dalai Lama that the United States was will-ing to provide aid to the Tibetan guerillas, but that the Americans wanted to know the Dalai Lama's intentions. The Dalai Lama said that neither he nor his cabinet had reached any decisions, but disclosed his intentions of setting up a temporary government at Luntze Dzong.

A HUNTED MAN

Soon after the conversation, the Dalai Lama and his party resumed their trek to the south. During the week that followed, travel included crossing mountains as high as 19,000 feet. When they came to E-Chhudhogyang, they understood the old Tibetan proverb about the place: "It's better to be born an animal in a place where there is grass and water than to be born in E-Chhudhogyang."[5] The desolate territory suffers perennial gales and storms, and its ground is ash-colored sand, where no grass or trees can grow. Although the townspeople were stone-poor, they welcomed party members into their homes and barns, for which the travelers were extremely grateful.

At about this time, the Dalai Lama's disappearance had hit world news-papers, and Zhou En-lai announced the liquidation of the Tibetan gov-ernment and its replacement by the provisional committee. Historical Tibet was no more, but the leader of the Chinese was unhappy. When told that the Dalai Lama had escaped, Chairman Mao said, "In that case we have lost the battle."[6] Mao ordered a major force of the PLA across the Tsangpo River to find the Dalai Lama.

Two days later, the refugees reached Luntze Dzong, where the people held a ceremony of thanksgiving for the Dalai Lama's safety. Afterward, he repudiated the Seventeen-Point Agreement, telling his people that the Chinese were no more than an invading power. Over a thousand people at-tended the ceremony of consecration over his newly formed government-in-exile, the only true government of Tibet. The speech was made on Tibetan soil, acknowledging his return and establishing Tibet's importance as an independent nation under siege. He also wanted to prove to the Ti-betan people that although he was no longer among them, he would always be with them. The monks of the fort handed the traditional seals of office to him, and all monks present chanted prayers over the Dalai Lama's reen-thronement. The Dalai Lama then signed a proclamation declaring the new government, copies of which would be distributed throughout Tibet. At this point, the Dalai Lama knew he had taken positive steps for Tibet's future.

Though the Dalai Lama had planned these actions as a permanent so-lution, his time at the fort would be short. News came of Chinese troop movements, and as Luntze Dzong was likely to be a prime target, the Dalai

Lama and his party had to quickly head out for the Indian border. Messengers were sent ahead to ask the government of India for asylum. They were told to give their request to the nearest official, who could forward the message to the Indian capital of New Delhi. They were to wait for the reply, and bring it back to the Dalai Lama as quickly as possible.

Though India was only a week's journey ahead, the last part of the expedition was the most grueling. At one junction, three different routes with varying degrees of difficulty led to India. To avoid complete capture, the group decided to split up and send members in each direction. The Dalai Lama's three ministers and his tutors took a lower mountain pass, which was longer than the others; some of the soldiers went a second way; the Dalai Lama chose the third option—another high pass.

Near the top of the mountain, the Dalai Lama and his companions ran into another blizzard. The air was so cold that ice formed on their eyelashes and eyebrows. The ponies were tired and hungry due to lack of vegetation in the frozen ground, and the only way to get them across the pass was to walk. Beyond the pinnacle, the travelers stopped to rest and have a meal of bread, hot water, and condensed milk; the meager rations more than satisfied the weary Tibetans.

When the Dalai Lama's party finally reached Jhora, they met up again with the Dalai Lama's mother and sister, who had traveled so quickly that they were able to spend two days at their estate, which had been awarded to the family at the Dalai Lama's enthronement. The advisors, tutors, and soldiers all met there at about the same time. Everyone spent the night, but continued their journey at four the next morning.

When the mountains began to climb again, the travelers headed into another storm, blowing snow whipping around their faces. Very few of them had eyewear to protect them from snow blindness, so they used their long hair braids or strips of cloth to keep their eyes covered.

More startling was the sound they heard at the crest of the pristine mountain—a twin-engine airplane, flying just two hundreds yards over their heads. On the gleaming white snow, the party was highly prominent, especially due to their red horse blankets. The Dalai Lama shouted for them to turn the blankets over to the duller side, and everyone jumped from their horses and scattered and crouched behind boulders or in dark patches where the snow had blown away. The plane flew over them so quickly that they never saw its markings, but they were certain it was a Chinese plane, since the airspace above Tibet was protected. The group thought they had been spotted. Worried about imminent capture, they continued their travel but split into smaller parties.

By noon that same day, they were again on flat land, when a dust storm rose up around them. Further along, on a wide plain, they found deep snow, and again needed to protect their eyes from snow blindness. But soon the messengers they had sent to India returned to delight them, as the Indian government had agreed to grant the Dalai Lama and all with him asylum.

LEAVING TIBET

The Dalai Lama's last night in Tibet was spent at Mangmang, the final settlement before the Indian border. The town seemed very safe, with only one well-protected track leading in and out. The Dalai Lama, however, was not comfortable. The party had to sleep in tents, and that night, the region suffered torrential downpours. The Dalai Lama's tent leaked, and water ran in rivulets down all sides. No matter where he moved his bedding, he was soaked, and he sat up, awake, during most of the night.

The stress and exhaustion turned into a high fever and a full-blown case of dysentery by the next morning. Because the Dalai Lama was too ill to travel, they moved him to a small house, which afforded a little more protection than the tent. The house was filthy with a residue of black smoke. Cows below his room lowed throughout the night and day, their stench rose from the ground floor to make his illness even more unbearable. In the morning, cocks crowed from the rafters above him.

On the second day at Mangmang, while lingering in misery, he heard a report from All-India Radio disclosing his intention to come to India. The report also said that he had fallen from his horse and was badly injured. The Dalai Lama laughed at the statement, since falling from his horse was about the only indignity he had not suffered along the way.

The next day, although still not fully recovered, the Dalai Lama knew he had to move on to relieve the rear guard of guerrillas protecting him. Fighters also reported that the Chinese were closing on Tsona, a village within striking distance of the camp. Although it pained him to say goodbye to the freedom fighters who had accompanied him on the journey, the Dalai Lama knew that—ailing or not—he had to move on. As he was still too ill to ride a horse, he rode on the back of a dzomo, which has an easy gait. In a haze of illness and in deep sorrow, he crossed the frontier into freedom on March 31, 1959.

The Dalai Lama's despondency and health improved when he reached the first towns and villages in India. An official and an interpreter greeted him and his party warmly, and they all continued on to Bomdila, where, three weeks after leaving Lhasa, he received a telegram of welcome from Indian Prime Minister Nehru.

The Dalai Lama remained in Bomdila for about ten days, while fully re-covering from his dysentery. On April 19, he was taken to Foothills, a road camp where an honor guard waited for him. That afternoon, he would go to Tezpur, and from there, he would begin his journey to Mus-soorie, where he and the other Tibetans would set up a new home. A train waited to transport them on the 1,500-mile journey.

As he left Foothills, the Dalai Lama saw several cameramen from the international press, who had come to report what they called the "story of the century." He was warned that he would see many more in Tezpur, where a larger contingent of newspeople awaited his arrival.

At Circuit House in Tezpur, the Dalai Lama met up with his brother Gyalo Thondup. He also found thousands of messages, telegrams, and letters waiting for him, and a huge contingent of reporters from all over the world. He prepared a short statement, outlining the history of the ordeal leading up to his flight, which was presented by a Tibetan official. In his message, he revealed for the first time that the Seventeen-Point Agreement was signed under duress and that from the day of the PLA's arrival in Lhasa, Tibet had been anything but autonomous. He denied the Chinese claim that he had been abducted, and stated emphatically that he had left Tibet of his own free will. He expressed grief over the tragedy in Lhasa and fervent wishes for the trouble to be over without further bloodshed.

China's reaction came quickly. The Xinhua News Agency reported that the Dalai Lama had been kidnapped and held against his will by the rebels, and implied that the kidnappers had acted under the orders of Tai-wan, Britain, the United States, and India. It further stated that "The so-called statement of the Dalai Lama ... is a crude document, lame in reasoning, full of lies and loopholes,"[7] insisting that the so-called Tibetan independence was a fabrication of the British to facilitate aggression to-ward both China and Tibet, and that since the document had been pre-sented in the third person, it was obviously not the Dalai Lama's composition.

The Tibetan question left Nehru in a delicate position. He dismissed the idea that India had any part in the Tibetan rebellion. He claimed that a huge segment of the Indian population felt sympathy for Tibet, and by offering the Dalai Lama asylum, he satisfied their discontent over Chinese reprisals there. He stressed that his support of the Dalai Lama was purely humanitarian and that the Dalai Lama was not permitted to use India as a base to pursue Tibetan independence. Nehru tried to keep the Dalai Lama from the press in order to soften the blow to the Chinese, but his ef-forts failed.

After the Tezpur speech had been presented, the Dalai Lama had lunch and set off for the train to Mussoorie, which was to depart at one o'clock. Thousands of well-wishers were at the train to meet him, and as the train continued along its route, people flocked to see him. He addressed people at different stops along the way, and was grateful for the warm welcome the Indian people showed him.

Another welcome awaited the Dalai Lama at Dera Dun. After three days of travel, only eighteen miles and an hour more by car separated him from his new home, known as Birla House. The residence had belonged to one of India's leading industrial families, and was built in the style of an English country manor. The house had two stories; a prominent veranda; and a terraced garden with lilies, blue and white violets, and irises.

Surrounding the property was a fourteen-foot-high barbed-wire fence. This and a contingent of security guards kept the Dalai Lama safe from unwanted visitors and the press, which the Indian government wanted as far away from the Dalai Lama as possible.

REPRIMAND AND CONFUSION

Nehru arrived in Mussoorie on April 24, and he and the Dalai Lama conferred for four hours. The Dalai Lama related all that had happened to him since his return to Tibet following the Buddha Jayanti. The Dalai Lama explained that he had dealt fairly and honestly with the Chinese and had not originally intended to seek asylum in India, but to establish his exile government at Luntze Dzong. He said that only after hearing the news of the carnage in Lhasa had he changed his mind.

The Indian prime minister was distressed over these last admissions. He retorted that even if the Dalai Lama had established a separate government outside Lhasa, the Indian government would not have recognized it. To the twenty-four-year-old Dalai Lama, Nehru's tone made his words sound like a reprimand. Nehru banged his fist on the table often, and became agitated by the Dalai Lama's disclosures.

Even in the face of Nehru's displeasure, the Dalai Lama continued: "I am determined to win independence for Tibet, but the immediate requirement is to put a stop to the bloodshed."[8]

At this, Nehru spat back, "You say you want independence and in the same breath you say you do not want bloodshed. Impossible!"[9]

Nehru's position in his own country was fragile regarding the situation in Tibet. For years, the Indian parliament had criticized him for mishandling the problem. On this day, Nehru learned that the Dalai Lama blamed him for insisting on his return to Tibet and reconciliation with the Chinese. Nehru's rationale was adherence to the Five Principles of Peaceful Coexistence memorandum of 1954—a trade agreement between China and India, which proclaimed India's acceptance of Tibet as part of China. Using it as his stanchion, Nehru made it clear that India would not take Tibet's side against China. He told the Dalai Lama not to make plans for the immediate future, as they would talk again.

When Nehru left, the Dalai Lama was confused by Nehru's words. Still, acknowledging the prime minister's delicate position, the Dalai Lama opted to take Nehru's advice and allow time for consideration.

Soon after arriving at Mussoorie, reports came about the thousands of refugees arriving in India and Bhutan from Tibet. Tibetans from every region had reacted quickly, as some 87,000 people had been killed in the Lhasa area alone. Many were desperate to leave Tibet to avoid Chinese "democratic reforms," including collectivization of property and labor, daily "reeducation," abolishment of the clergy, class division, an influx of Chinese settlers, and possible death. Tibetans who crossed borders did so impulsively and in a state of abject deprivation.

In India, two camps were organized for the refugees—one at Missamari and another at Buxa Duar, a former British prisoner-of-war camp in West Bengal. The Indian people joined in procuring food, medical supplies, and clothing for the refugees.

Yet the camps proved inadequate, as the Tibetans could not adjust to the climate. Whereas Mussoorie, at six thousand feet, had a tolerable cool climate, both refugee camps were at lower elevations and the heat was unbearable for Tibetans, who were used to life amid the Himalayas. High temperatures were often fatal to them, as were illnesses. Because viruses expire at high altitudes, Tibetans had never been exposed to them. In the lower-sited Indian camps, viruses flourished, and many Tibetans, with no immunities to disease, died.

In June, the Dalai Lama traveled to New Delhi to speak with Prime Minister Nehru once again. He begged that the refugee camps be moved to cooler altitudes. About twenty thousand refugees were in the camps at the time, including women and children.[10] The Dalai Lama explained that if they were left in Missamari and Buxa Duar, a majority of them would die.

Nehru told the Dalai Lama that he asked too much and needed to realize that India was a poor, developing country. However, he agreed to send the Tibetan refugees to road camps in northern India, higher up, and to make the arrangements as soon as possible. In these camps, the people would help build roads and have a better chance of survival in more hospitable climates.

Nehru then surprised the Dalai Lama by addressing the needs of Tibetan children. Nehru said they should have separate schools in order to preserve Tibetan heritage, and readily agreed to establish an independent Society for Tibetan Education, for which the Indian government would bear all expenses, along with the expense of setting up the schools. He cautioned the Dalai Lama that the children should be thoroughly educated on the culture and tradition of Tibet but also the modern world. The Dalai Lama, as a progressive Tibetan, agreed wholeheartedly. Nehru proposed that the language used in the schools be English, as it would one day be the international language. The Dalai Lama agreed.

A NEW TIBET IN EXILE

After returning to Mussoorie, the Dalai Lama held a press conference. Although the story of his reaching India was old news by then, 130 reporters—representing nations from around the world—still flocked to hear him speak. The Dalai Lama's statement formally repudiated the Seventeen-Point Agreement once again, and explained that since China herself had broken the accord, there was no longer a legal basis for its recognition.

He also told reporters of atrocities suffered by the Tibetan people at the hands of the Chinese, and stated his belief that their intent was not only to eradicate Tibetan religion and culture, but to completely absorb the Tibetan race. He also stated that the government of Tibet was with him, regardless of his location, and that he would not return to Tibet until conditions returned to those prior to the Chinese intervention.

That night, a rapid communiqué came from the Indian government, stating emphatically that they did not recognize the Dalai Lama's government-in-exile. The statement was a blow to the Dalai Lama even though he knew why it had been made—the Indian government needed to gain some distance in order to avoid conflict with China—and he recognized the act as true democracy in action. Whereas the Indian government disputed his point of view, they did nothing to stop him from expressing it.

The Dalai Lama leaned closer to democracy rather than socialism at Birla House, and many protocols changed there as well. He gave weekly audiences for people from all over the world. He insisted that all formality be significantly reduced, demanded that people not perform the old courtesies, and thought the new attitude was especially important when dealing with non-Tibetans. He stipulated chairs of equal height for all, doing away with the old practice of keeping himself above all others. He wanted to be open and have people relate to him as a human being rather than as a god-king. This seemed awkward at first, but the Dalai Lama soon learned to enjoy his "equal" status.

Thubten Jigme Norbu came to visit the Dalai Lama and the rest of his family for one of the Dalai Lama's weekly audiences and was shocked at the new attitude.

> I was about to prostrate myself before him, as I had always been ac-customed to do, and to present the usual kata, when with a gesture of the hand he indicated that I should not do so here. Wordlessly he pointed to a [sacred cloth painting] with the picture of Buddha Shakyamuni; and deeply moved I laid my good-luck scarf over it. Henceforth our reverential greetings were to honour the Buddhas alone; from now on, the Dalai Lama regarded himself only as the first fugitive amongst his oppressed people.[11]

Birla House lent itself well to a reduction in protocol, especially since the Dalai Lama shared the house with his mother, Tendzin Choegyal, and Tsering Dolma and her husband, who had returned from Taiwan. The Dalai Lama enjoyed being with the family for extended periods. They walked in the gardens and watched movies together, and for the first time in his life, the Dalai Lama carried on a normal relationship with them.

As the governmental organization was also much less formal, the Dalai Lama found it easier to create governmental departments he had found lacking in Tibet. He established the offices of information, education, re-habilitation, security, religious affairs, and economic affairs, and encour-aged women to take part in government. He stressed that positions should always be filled based on ability rather than gender.

In September 1959, the Dalai Lama returned to New Delhi. By this time, thirty thousand refugees had arrived in India, but Nehru had stayed true to his word and had already placed many Tibetans in road camps in northern India. However, the welfare of Tibetan exiles was not the objec-tive of this visit. He wanted a hearing on Tibet at the United Nations.

Nehru was not amenable to promoting such a request. Since neither Tibet nor China were members of the United Nations, it seemed un-likely that such a request would be honored. He told the Dalai Lama that even if he succeeded in obtaining a hearing, not much would come of it. The Dalai Lama replied that while he realized that all of that was true, he was convinced that he needed to keep the plight of Tibet before the world.

Ignoring Nehru's warning, the Dalai Lama went about meeting with ambassadors from many nations. Some were sympathetic and advised him on how to proceed. Ultimately, the Republic of Ireland and the Federation of Malaya sponsored a draft resolution, which was to be debated before the General Assembly in October. The Dalai Lama was satisfied that at last, the world would be aware of the plight of his people.

NOTES

1. Quoted in Avedon, *In Exile from the Land of Snows*, p. 55.
2. Ibid. p. 56.
3. Ibid.
4. Ibid., p. 57.
5. The Dalai Lama of Tibet, *My Land and My People*, p. 171.
6. Quoted in Tenzin Gyatso, *Freedom in Exile*, p. 221.
7. Quoted in Avedon, *In Exile from the Land of Snows*, p. 68.
8. Tenzin Gyatso, *Freedom in Exile*, p. 147.
9. Quoted in Tenzin Gyatso, *Freedom in Exile*, p. 147.
10. Over time, their numbers would swell to 100,000.
11. Thubten Jigme Norbu and Heinrich Harrer, *Tibet Is My Country*, p. 251.

Chapter 9

A MORE PERMANENT HOME

The year 1959 was a time of change, even outside Tibet and India. Fidel Castro took control of Cuba, Hawaii became the fiftieth U.S. state, and the Soviet Union launched its first monkey-manned rocket. None of these history-making events would have any impact on Tibetan refugees teeming into India by the thousands. Neither did the world mourn with Tibetans over the loss of their homeland.

In October, discussions about Tibet proceeded at the United Nations' Fourteenth General Assembly, but the results were not as satisfying as the Dalai Lama had hoped. Communist countries were quick to insist that Tibet belonged to China and that the assembly had no right to even discuss the situation, let alone intervene. The UN ambassador from the USSR cited the Cold War[1] as the underlying cause of this concern over China's internal problems, and accused the appeal's sponsors of using the UN to incite conflict. As this confrontation was something the capitalist nations—including the United States and Great Britain—had wanted to avoid, the question of Tibet's autonomy was shelved due to the global atmosphere of the time.

Instead, the assembly focused on the denial of human rights, and a resolution was adopted, which stated that UN members were: "Gravely concerned at reports, including the official statements of His Holiness the Dalai Lama, to the effect that the fundamental human rights and freedoms of the people of Tibet have been forcibly denied them" and called for "respect for the fundamental human rights of the Tibetan people and for their distinctive cultural and religious life."[2]

Although the resolution was better than total apathy regarding Tibet, it was ineffective, as the Chinese seemed to disregard world opinion. The resolution was hardly what the Tibetans needed or wanted, but it was the most that they could achieve.

CARING FOR THE POPULATION

Back at Mussoorie, the Dalai Lama continued to give his weekly audiences and sent his older brother to the road camps to assess the well-being of the refugees. Thubten Jigme Norbu also traveled to Switzerland to finalize a plan, initiated by the Dalai Lama, to transport Tibetan refugee children to the Pestalozzi Children's Village for war orphans, which had been founded during World War II. Other Pestalozzi camps were open in Britain, France, and Germany, so Thubten Jigme Norbu traveled to those countries as well, in order to broaden the government-in-exile's options.

To help the refugees in Darjeeling, Gyalo Thondup's wife set up a Tibetan Self-Help Center. The center's shops allowed Tibetans to pursue the traditional arts and crafts of Tibet and maintain employment as salespeople or craftspeople. As with work on the road crews, the center made it possible for refugees to earn money, but even more importantly, it helped exiled Tibetans regain self-respect. While providing a small income for their families, they were helping to preserve Tibetan culture. With the program's success, many such centers sprang up throughout the Tibetan-inhabited areas of India.

Meanwhile, the Dalai Lama anguished over his lack of power to improve conditions in the refugee camps. Of Missamari and Buxa Duar, the latter camp was the less hospitable. Its residents—most of which were monks and lamas—were housed in thirty concrete barracks, surrounded by barbed-wire fences. The conditions were unwholesome; many of the monks died from cholera, dysentery, malaria, and hepatitis. They had no electricity, so kerosene lamps were brought in to provide enough light to read scriptures by, which subjected the monks to toxic fumes from the burning fuel. Many contracted tuberculosis; many died.

Although conditions for Tibetans throughout India were not ideal, the Dalai Lama had come to accept that there would be no quick return to Tibet and that his people had chosen to suffer the conditions of exile rather than returning to a Tibet ruled by China.

The Dalai Lama's advisors sought donations and negotiated with the government of India to help the refugees. Yet a great deal of the work involved in developing a long-term strategy fell to the Dalai Lama. Because he was so wise and learned, most outsiders wanted to deal with him directly. His renown was essential in establishing goodwill among nations and with philanthropic entities. He worked tirelessly to inform the world about Tibet, hoping that the plight of his country would strike individuals, who would aid in Tibet's struggle with China. He also wanted to look toward establishing a nontraditional government once Tibet was set free.

A NEW DIRECTION

Although he had earlier leaned toward Marxism and socialism, the Dalai Lama realized that democracy was the best option after seeing how well the system worked in India. He speculated that democracy was key to survival in a modern world, and so pushed for a constitution.

He proposed a presidential system in which the Dalai Lama would be head of state. The cabinet was to be appointed, and would be free to address the congress but not to vote. He advocated the right of the congress to remove a minister and the right of the supreme court to step in should the Dalai Lama and the congress ever come to odds. The Dalai Lama's plan met with some resistance, but a second plan was in utter opposition to Tibetan tradition: "The Dalai Lama himself should be subject to the deprivation of his powers, in the highest interests of the state, by legislative and judicial processes to be prescribed in the constitution."[3] His advisors were outraged by this proposal, and would not allow the provision to be made part of the Tibetan Constitution. Steeped in Tibetan policies and politics, their rigidness would be difficult to overcome, but the Dalai Lama was determined to change not only their mind-set but also the traditions of his people.

In December 1959, the Dalai Lama went among the Tibetan exiles to prepare them for the transitions he wanted to make. He knew that Tibet had failed with China, not only because of its isolationist stance but also because of its inability to move ahead in time. By changing attitudes of both government-in-exile leaders and refugees, the Dalai Lama knew his plan would lead to hope and give his people courage to continue in their new land.

At Buddhist shrines, he provided public teachings. At a Tibetan monastery within sight of the Bodhi Tree, under which Buddha obtained enlightenment, he met with sixty refugees who pledged to continue the fight to win Tibet's freedom and independence. Then, for the first time in his life and in the first rite since coming to India, he performed the ordination of one hundred sixty-two monks.

In the Deer Park at Sarnath, where Buddha had preached his first sermon, the Dalai Lama addressed two thousand refugees, who had recently arrived in India by way of Nepal. They camped beneath the trees and set up stalls to sell what little they had—clothing, meager valuables, and mainly tea. The Dalai Lama was touched by their ability to make the best of difficult times.

For two weeks he preached to people from all provinces of Tibet, first in the traditional Tibetan manner—from a high throne—and then in the less formal advisory manner in which he wanted to address his people in the future. He presented long-range plans for the reconstruction of Tibetan life in India and for the continued struggle to regain Tibet, and showed how the two would combine. "For the moment Tibet's sun and moon have suffered an eclipse," he told them, "but one day we will regain our country. You should not lose heart. The great job ahead of us now is to preserve our religion and culture."[4] He reminded them of Buddha's words when he said that suffering is the first step toward liberation—or, in the words of an old Tibetan adage, "Pain is what you measure pleasure by."

ACCEPTING CONDITIONS

Soon after returning to Mussoorie, the Dalai Lama learned that he was to move to another, larger home in Dharamsala, and he found the news disquieting. A hill station, like Mussoorie, Dharamsala was even more remote and a whole day's journey from the Indian capital of New Delhi. He worried that the Indian government wanted to hide him from the world in order to maintain their tentative relations with China.

The Dalai Lama asked the Indian government to allow a representative to scout the new location before they moved their camp, hoping to dissuade the government's plans if the accommodations were not suitable. However, a member of the Dalai Lama's cabinet viewed the spot and, upon his return to Mussoorie, told the Dalai Lama that Dharamsala was a much better place. Immediate plans were made for relocation.

While preparations were underway, the Dalai Lama visited the road camps in northern India, where thousands of Tibetans were engaged in road building. He was distressed by the sight of Tibetan men, women, and children working alongside monks and nuns from various monasteries. He knew that after a long day of working under the tireless sun, they would be crammed into tents at night to sleep, and although cooler than the camps at Missamari and Buxa Duar, the climate was still oppressive and continued to be the cause of many Tibetan deaths.

The work was dangerous as well. Dynamite, used to level steep mountainsides, claimed many Tibetan lives, as did bug bites, especially those of malaria-carrying mosquitoes. Many people suffered serious illness or were maimed or crippled. But despite their torment, the Tibetans were steadfastly loyal to the Dalai Lama, showed him deep respect, and valiantly responded to his plea to remain optimistic. Although the Dalai Lama had been raised to expect such devotion, sensing his people's intense physical and emotional pain, the Dalai Lama was overwhelmed by their fervor toward him.

The children, however, worried him. He saw their bodies wracked by malnutrition, and immediately contacted the Indian government to implore its help. The Indians quickly responded and set up a new camp, specifically designed to serve the special needs of the Tibetan children. At the same time, fifty children were sent to Mussoorie, where the first Tibetan school had been established.

Some progress had been made since the Dalai Lama's arrival in India, less than a year ago. On the anniversary of his flight from Tibet, he established a new precedent for speaking publicly about the Tibetan uprising and the state of Tibet. In his first speech, he stressed the need for the Tibetan people still in Tibet to consider their country's struggle a long-term project. For the exiles, he stated that resettlement and the maintenance of Tibetan culture were their duties. He also gave his people hope when he declared that through truth, justice, and courage, Tibet would one day regain its freedom.

The following month, the Dalai Lama left Mussoorie for his new home in Dharamsala via overnight train and motorcade. Along the way, he was impressed by the Indian countryside, where trees dotted the lush green landscape and wildflowers bloomed in magnificent color. Almost twenty-four hours later, the traveling party arrived at Dharamsala, where the Dalai Lama exchanged his limousine for a Jeep. His new house was situated just above the town of McLeod Ganj, which overlooked a broad valley.

Outside the compound, a new bamboo gate had been erected, and the word "Welcome" was painted in gold letters across its top. After another mile, he arrived at Swarg Ashram. Formerly known as Highcroft House, it had been the residence of the divisional commissioner during the British occupation of India. The small house was situated in the woods and surrounded by a compound of outbuildings, including three houses to accommodate his officials. Although the camp was smaller than the Dalai Lama had anticipated, the view of the wondrous, familiar Himalayan mountains made him happy to be settled permanently in a new home.

TESTIMONY TO SUFFERING

Two weeks after his arrival, the Dalai Lama opened the first nursery for Tibetan refugee children and appointed his sister Tsering Dolma as its head. Although the orphanage was thought to be small for the first influx of 50 children, it became even smaller when the number rose to 500 and the children kept coming. They had to sleep lying crosswise, with five or six to a bed, and at one point, 120 children had to share a single bedroom. Although they were living under less than perfect circumstances and without parents, the Dalai Lama took delight in their apparent ability to make the best of a bad situation and loved to hear their laughter and to watch them play.

Yet it soon became apparent that some of the children would have to be given up for adoption—in Europe. The Dalai Lama spoke with the head of the Pestalozzi Children's Village, who got the Swiss government to take two hundred of the children immediately. Although the Tibetan children would be adopted by Swiss families, they were guaranteed the right to pursue their Tibetan culture and identity. Later, older children were sent to Switzerland to study and one thousand adult refugees were provided the means for resettlement there.[5]

Just before his arrival at Dharamsala, the Dalai Lama also spoke with the International Commission of Jurists (ICJ), which had invited him to give testimony regarding the Tibetan plight. In August 1960, a report was issued, finding the Tibetan claims to be well-founded. It read in part:

The allegations against the People's Republic of China can be fitted into three broad legal categories:

1) Systematic disregard for the obligations under the Seventeen-Point Agreement of 1951;

2) Systematic violation of the fundamental rights and freedoms of the people of Tibet;

3) Wanton killing of Tibetans and other acts capable of leading to the extinction of the Tibetans as a national and religious group, to the extent that it becomes necessary to consider the question of genocide.[6]

The Tibetans were encouraged by the report, though the ICJ was not working for Tibet or for the Dalai Lama. An independent association of judges, lawyers, and legal teachers, the ICJ is supported by 300,000 lawyers from 50 different countries and examines all systematic violations of the rule of law—wherever they exist. The commission looked at the Tibetan situation only out of their charter obligation to do so.

During its evaluation, the ICJ took into consideration statements the Dalai Lama had made on June 20, 1959, at Mussoorie:

The ultimate Chinese aim with regard to Tibet, as far as I can make out, seems to attempt the extermination of religion and culture and even the absorption of the Tibetan race.... Besides the civilian and military personnel already in Tibet, five million Chinese settlers have arrived in eastern and north-eastern Tso, in addition to which four million Chinese settlers are planned to be sent to U and Sung provinces of Central Tibet. Many Tibetans have been deported, thereby resulting in the complete absorption of these Tibetans as a race, which is being undertaken by the Chinese.[7]

Among other crimes, the ICJ accused the Chinese of genocide, of deterring the practice of Buddhism and intending its eradication, of torture and inhuman treatment, and of denying Tibetans the right to freedom of thought.

PROMOTING ESTABLISHMENT

The Dalai Lama prepared himself for an apathetic response to the report; however, his testimony had a beneficial side effect. One of the jurists asked the Dalai Lama whether the Tibetans in exile had monitored Peking radio broadcasts, and was shocked to learn that they had not. He told the Dalai Lama that they should do so immediately and warned that it was necessary to listen very closely to what was being said. The Dalai Lama immediately understood the import of the practice, as the broadcasts would lead to an indication of Chinese policy. He ordered his cabinet to set to this task rightaway.

He also continued the process of turning his government-in-exile into a democratic machine. On September 2, he inaugurated the Commission of Tibetan People's Deputies, which would become the Tibetan congress. He made membership open to freely elected representatives from all three regions of Tibet—U-Tsang, Kham, and Amdo. Each of the Buddhist schools also had seats, later including those from the Bön tradition. Many were unhappy with the Dalai Lama's new reforms, and even accused him of practicing true Communism. Yet the Dalai Lama stayed true to his mission, and to this day, strives to improve the system of democracy he envisions.

Above governmental concerns, the Dalai Lama wanted to concentrate on preserving Buddhism. He persuaded the Indian government to provide for a community of three hundred monks at Buxa Duar; however, the environment at the camp continued to be severe. In addition to the disease and death, food rations, which had to be shipped very long distances to reach them, often arrived spoiled. The Dalai Lama knew how hard conditions were, but could only send taped messages and letters to buoy their spirits.[8]

A lack of funds was a major concern for the Dalai Lama. Although the Indian government had been very generous in their support of Tibetan education and resettlement, the Dalai Lama did not feel it was right to ask for money for administration. A voluntary freedom tax of two rupees per person per month did not raise much revenue, nor did a 2 percent tax on the salary of working people, which was also voluntary. Yet the treasure boxes, stored in Sikkim since 1950, were still intact, and after much discussion about their disposition, the contents were sold on the open market at Calcutta for $8 million.

Tibetans made investments, hoping to increase the amount of wealth, as $8 million was not enough to run a government. Ventures in an iron pipe manufacturing plant and a paper mill failed, and officials responsible for watching the treasury embezzled some of the money. A majority of the capital was lost, but the Tibetans struggled on, trying to make their way in an unfamiliar world. Although they were changing due to the foresight of the Dalai Lama, even he had not realized the pitfalls outside Tibet.

For China, the worst consequence of the Tibetan revolt was its deteriorating relations with India. For India, the uprising proved how unstable the plateau of central Asia actually was, and presented the country with a new danger—from its border, which was no longer controlled by Tibet but by China.

The year 1962 saw a change in Prime Minister Nehru, as well. Although he had stood on the side of China's right to hold suzerainty over Tibet and had encouraged the Dalai Lama to continue negotiating with the Chinese, at a time when negotiations were pointless, he finally saw proof that the Tibetans were not to blame in the events of 1959.

By 1962, India began to worry over the concentration of PLA troops near its border. China saw India's aid to Tibetan refugees and the Dalai Lama as no less than collusion, and diplomatic relations between India and China deteriorated on several fronts, especially that of the boundary line between India and what had been Tibet. When the debate heated, Indian troops were sent to the border, and they skirmished with Chinese forces sporadically for ten months. On October 20, China crossed the McMahon Line, named for the British negotiator during the Simla Conference, when the borders were set between India and Tibet. The ill-equipped and inexperienced Indian army was essentially defeated in the short war, although the Chinese called a unilateral cease-fire on November 21, when India sought the help of the United States.

U.S. President John F. Kennedy was quick to offer military assistance, and only then did India learn that the Americans had been aiding the Tibetans. Nehru suddenly recognized the benefit of having the Dalai Lama and the Tibetans in India, and policies toward the refugees changed dramatically. The Indian government adopted a program that was supportive to the Dalai Lama's government-in-exile, allocated more land for resettlement, and increased aid to refugee rehabilitation.

India and the United States also approved a joint venture to support the military base in Mustang, Nepal, where CIA-trained guerrilla fighters set off for clandestine operations inside Tibet—a program established largely due to the work of Gyalo Thondup. The arrangement worked tentatively until 1963, when the attention of India and the United States were directed elsewhere.

For India, the exiled Tibetans represented a potentially stronger military force, which gave them greater security in case of Chinese border offensives. For its part, the CIA no longer saw China as the main threat to its Asian interests. The Soviet Union now concerned America, owing to Cuba's fealty to the Communist nation and the fact that Cuba was only ninety miles away from Key West, Florida.

However, as early as 1961, the United States was losing interest in the Tibetan project. In a memorandum from the United States ambassador to India to the undersecretary of state for economic affairs, the ambassador wrote: "It was once thought that the operations would keep the Chinese from consolidating their hold on Tibet. Of this there is no chance.... by keeping alive the resistance, the Chinese aggression in Tibet is kept before world opinion.... the truth is that the operation continues because it got started. This argument holds in effect that we must inherit and carry out faithfully the mistakes of the previous Administration."[9]

From that time onward, U.S. cooperation for the project was in decline, and by the mid-1960s the CIA met only a fraction of the Mustang operation's costs. In 1965, the United States told the Tibetans that it would continue to reduce their funding until stopping it altogether in 1968.

For the Dalai Lama, Mustang became somewhat of an embarrassment. The king of Nepal had died in 1972, and though he had ignored Tibetan activities in his country, his son, and successor, did not. He wanted to ally more strongly with China and found the Tibetans intolerable. By 1973, the Nepalese government ordered the Tibetans to lay down their weapons and to disband the Mustang base, but after long years of fighting, they were not so easily discouraged. They refused to surrender their weapons readily, but said they would do so in increments, over a three-year period.

Because the Dalai Lama preached nonviolence and had achieved a measure of respect in the world for his policies, he saw this refusal to cooperate as potentially damaging to Tibet's international reputation. His prime minister took a recorded message from him to Mustang and played it to the men, whose devotion to the Dalai Lama made them realize that they had no choice but to surrender their weapons.

But empathy for Tibet's situation had turned to apathy in the world court by 1973. The fact that China had ruled the country for twenty-two years had transformed the plight of Tibet, the independent nation, into an internal issue for a province of China—a civil war. Yet the Dalai Lama continued to stress his government-in-exile, and although he represented his trip as a religious pilgrimage, he had other purposes in mind when he set off for the West.

NOTES

1. A term used to refer to the state of military and political rivalry between communists and capitalists, which continued from the mid-1940s until the breakup of the Soviet bloc.

2. United Nations General Assembly, *Resolution 1353 (XIV)*, 1959, http://www.tibet.com/Resolution/un59.html.

3. The Dalai Lama of Tibet, *My Land and My People*, p. 194.

4. Quoted in John F. Avedon, *In Exile from the Land of Snows*, p. 82.

5. The Dalai Lama was extremely grateful to the Swiss government, and he saw to it that as the Tibetan situation in India improved, the Swiss government would no longer be relied on for assistance.

6. International Commission of Jurists, *The Question of Tibet*, Geneva, 1959.

7. Ibid.

8. Eventually, the survivors of Buxa Duar became the heart of a strong religious community.

9. Department of State, *Foreign Relations of the United States, 1961–1963, Vol. XXII, China; Korea; Japan*. (Washington D.C.: Government Printing Office).

Chapter 10

CHARMING THE WORLD

Before the squabble between Tibetan guerrillas and the Nepalese government came to a head in 1973, many events had changed the refugees' and the Dalai Lama's way of life in India. One major change for the Dalai Lama came when he saw the need to offer himself as goodwill ambassador for the Tibetan government-in-exile, primarily to get the message of Tibet's plight out to the world.

To introduce himself, the Dalai Lama published his autobiography, *My Land and My People*, in 1962. In this glimpse of his hidden life in Tibet, the Dalai Lama provided an account of the Chinese occupation, culminating in his exile. This effort threw the plight of his people and his country into the minds of millions—especially the Americans, who were quite interested in the mystical Dalai Lama.

Beginning with the beat generation in the 1950s, Buddhism had attracted high-profile supporters, such as poet Allen Ginsberg and author Jack Kerouac, and their followers promoted Buddhism in the United States. This only added to the Shangri-La mystique, and led to people's fascination with all things Tibetan. Through his book, the Dalai Lama hoped to erase misconceptions about his country and to show why his people needed support from the outside world.

In moving toward stability for his political ideals, the outline for the constitution of the Tibetan government-in-exile was presented to the Tibetan refugees for evaluation on March 10, 1963. In seventy-seven articles, the strong executive branch, headed by the Dalai Lama, was balanced with a congress and a judiciary. It stipulated the rights of Tibetans to include equality before the law; universal suffrage; and the right to life, liberty, and the freedoms of speech and religion. Although these were democratic ideals, the constitution also included socialist aims by providing for state ownership of the land and by prohibiting the amassing of wealth and the production of any product "to the common detriment." The constitution passed by general referendum.

Also in the early 1960s, twenty settlements for Tibetan refugees were established—largely in southern India—taking many Tibetans away from the road crews and restoring them to self-sufficiency. Although adjustment to the tropical climate presented a hardship for the Tibetans, the Dalai Lama remained certain that his people would adapt. He visited them often, explaining that the fate of Tibet rested on their resilience and tenacity, and stressing that the only way to preserve their culture and religion was by building strong communities, imparting proper education to their children, and reestablishing marriage and procreation as an important part of life.

With the Dalai Lama behind them, Tibetans in some settlements not only adapted but prospered. Other settlements were not so successful. Wild elephants and boars plagued one area, where crops were destroyed, homes were trampled, and several people died in a stampede. The Tibetans had no remedy for the problem until the Dalai Lama visited Switzerland several years later and noticed electronically fenced farms. When he learned that intensified voltage would stop elephants, he arranged to have enough fencing sent to India to solve the problem. However, not all quandaries were physical in nature.

At another settlement, the Tibetans balked at using fire to clear the land. Many small creatures had been destroyed while using this method, which was counter to the Buddhist ethic. Many settlers tried to have the work stopped; however, with no available alternatives, the effort had to continue for the welfare of the people.

All attempts at establishing poultry and pig farms, even under the auspices of overseas aid organizations, were unsuccessful, as Tibetans had never been involved in preparing animals for food. In urban Tibet, a thriving Muslim community had existed among the Buddhists, and since animal slaughter was not counter to Muslim religious beliefs, Muslims were the butchers. Although it is acceptable for Buddhists to eat prepared meat, it is not proper for them to take part in butchery.

"In rural areas," writes Professor Lee Feigon, "Tibetan herders often resort to subterfuges such as stuffing the mouths and nostrils of their animals with mud and leaving them to suffocate. When the Tibetans come back a few hours later to find their dead yak, the herders apparently have little difficulty in persuading themselves they might as well eat the carcasses rather than let them go to waste."[1] But even this practice was not possible on a large scale, and all attempts at animal farming failed. Still, the Tibetan people kept working to make their life in exile successful and tried to see each hardship as part of their karmic existence.

DEATH AND SUFFERING

Back in Dharamsala, a personal loss brought grief to the Dalai Lama and his family in November 1964, when his sister Tsering Dolma died of cancer at age forty-five. The Dalai Lama subsequently put twenty-three-year-old Jetsun Pema, who had worked closely with her sister, in charge of the Tibetan Children's Village. She saw the appointment as a substantial responsibility but also as a gift of love from her brother and sister. "Tsering Dolma had devoted her life to the children in exile. She had created from scratch the structures which had enabled hundreds to avoid almost certain death, and after the first urgent medical care, to receive little by little a sound education in a climate of love, tenderness and understanding."[2]

Another death in 1964 would have bearing on the Tibetan situation, as well. When Prime Minister Nehru died in May, a new prime minister—Lal Bahdur Shastri—took his place. Although disheartened over the death of his reluctant mentor, the Dalai Lama saw his replacement in a positive light. He had met Shastri several times and respected him greatly, yet Shastri's most potent characteristic was that he would be a better political ally than the man he replaced, leaning toward Tibet rather than China.

Prime Minister Shastri showed his allegiance in 1965, after the Chinese officially named eastern and central Tibet the Tibet Autonomous Region, and the United Nations once again discussed the plight of Tibet in the General Assembly. Shastri insisted that India vote on the side of Tibet, along with Thailand, the Philippines, Malta, Ireland, Nicaragua, El Salvador, and Malaysia. However, remaining countries considered the Chinese conquest of Tibet a fait accompli. Although Shastri's action accomplished little, it gave the Dalai Lama reason to believe that the Indian government might be of future assistance in the global arena and perhaps soon recognize Tibet's government-in-exile.

However, India's interest in Tibetan affairs was redirected in 1965, when India went to war with Pakistan for the second time over the Kashmir territory. What began as a series of border flare-ups resulted in mutual air assaults, and as Dharamsala lies less than one hundred miles from the India-Pakistan border, the fighting was close to the Dalai Lama's dwelling. However, he was not affected by the danger, as a regularly scheduled visit of Tibetan settlements took him away from Dharamsala to safety.

On his arrival, the Dalai Lama was pleased to find conditions improved at the settlement where the land-clearing dispute had arisen, although the community was by then home to 3,200 people. Permanent brick housing had been erected, wells had been drilled, and the land had finally been cleared for farming. Via the International Red Cross, most had medical care. Each person had been given one acre of land, although the settlers opted to farm the land collectively and keep only enough ground for small kitchen gardens near their homes. The Dalai Lama saw this as evidence of the benefits of determination. Although life was still extremely hard for the settlers, they were no longer hopeless.

After spending time with his countrymen, the Dalai Lama decided to take brief tours of three Indian cities and then set off for Trivandrum, the capital of the Indian state of Kerala. In Trivandrum, the Dalai Lama was invited to stay in the governor's residence, where his room overlooked the kitchen. When he witnessed a cook wringing a chicken's neck, he vowed to become a vegetarian.

This course of diet had been an impossible way of life in Tibet. Due to the hard mountain soil, which prevented produce farming, Tibet lacked vegetables. Along with tsampa, meat had always played an important role in Tibetan nutrition. In India, where vegetables were readily available, the Dalai Lama had no trouble refusing meat, eggs, and fish. His change of diets; however, was more than just a physical change; since vegetarianism is a strict interpretation of Mahayana Buddhist laws, the Dalai Lama also experienced spiritual fulfillment through his change of diet.

On January 10, 1966, India's war with Pakistan ended, but within hours of signing an agreement, Prime Minister Shastri was dead. The Dalai Lama lamented his death, as he viewed Shastri as a proactive and decisive leader. The possibility of Indian recognition of his government-in-exile was once again unresolved, and he had no guarantee that a new prime minister would take a similar stance to that of Shastri.

Two weeks later, the question of Indian leadership was fulfilled when Indira Gandhi—whose husband was no relation to Mahatma Gandhi— was sworn in as prime minister. She and the Dalai Lama had grown close over the years of Jawaharlal Nehru's power, as she was Nehru's daughter. The Dalai Lama was delighted at the turn of events. Mrs. Gandhi had been supportive of the Tibetan cause over the years, and had been an original member of the Tibetan Homes Foundation—a vocational center in Mussoorie that trains young Tibetans in traditional arts and crafts, allowing them to earn a livelihood later in life and to contribute to their community while preserving Tibetan traditions. The Dalai Lama was sure that Indira Gandhi would be a valuable ally, and as he wound up his Indian travels, improvements in conditions for Tibetan exiles on several fronts encouraged him.

Back in Dharamsala in 1966, the Dalai Lama took his vow of vegetarianism seriously. His cooks, unfamiliar with the preparation of vegetarian meals, had to remaster cooking for the Dalai Lama, but eventually, he was quite satisfied by their new recipes for Tibetan classic dishes. Owing to a lack of protein in the vegetarian diet, the Dalai Lama was counseled to drink milk and eat nuts as supplements, which he drank and ate in abundance.

Even so, the Dalai Lama contracted a severe case of jaundice. In addition to his skin turning bright yellow, he lost his appetite completely and fell into a state of total exhaustion. He suffered from hepatitis B, and was cured only after ingesting mass quantities of Tibetan medicines. His doctors insisted that he shun greasy foods and nuts, and that he start eating meat again. The doctors worried about permanent damage to his liver and said that the illness had probably shortened his life span. The Dalai Lama had no choice but to refute his earlier decision and return to an omnivorous diet.

REACHING OUT TO THE WORLD AND INTO HIMSELF

In 1967, the Dalai Lama became a world traveler, beginning with trips to Japan and Thailand in the autumn of that year. In 1968, he moved from Swarg Ashram to Bryn Cottage, on the grounds of McLeod-Ganj. Bryn Cottage was no larger than Swarg Ashram, but the new compound held an office for the Dalai Lama, a room where he could hold audiences, the private office of the government-in-exile, and the Indian Security Office. At the same time, his mother was moved to a residence of her own, which allowed the Dalai Lama to live a solitary monk's life once more.

The Dalai Lama's new accommodations suited him. He was thrilled with his private garden, and immediately set to planting many different types of trees and flowers. As a side benefit, the garden attracted animals and birds, which he had always loved.

He built a small bird table outside his study window, and surrounded it with netting to keep out large birds and birds of prey. The netting was not always successful, however, and the Dalai Lama often went for his air rifle to scare the big birds away. Although a proficient marksman—after years of practice with the Thirteenth Dalai Lama's guns at the Potala—he never wanted to harm the birds, just to frighten them away.

At Bryn Cottage, the Dalai Lama was able to settle into a routine, which included visiting the refugee settlements yearly, teaching, and continuing his religious studies. He also reacquired his enthusiasm for photography. At about age fourteen, he had begun taking pictures and had even constructed his own darkroom at the Norbulingka, where a Tibetan official taught him how to develop film.

He also resumed his avocation as tinkerer. He set aside a workroom and acquired a proper set of tools for working on watches. Although he was overwhelmingly successful in his technique, he claims to regret one irreparable watch, which belonged to a member of his government. He was forced to return it to its owner—in pieces.

Another interest of the Dalai Lama's while at Bryn Cottage was his cats. A black-and-white spotted cat was prized for her friendly nature; however, she could not resist the urge to chase mice—a bad occupation for a Buddhist's cat—and she often required disciplining. During her last episode, the cat vaulted to the top of a curtain when the Dalai Lama shouted at her. She lost her balance, fell, and did not survive the resultant injury.

The Dalai Lama's second cat was discovered in his garden as a kitten. Her hind legs were crippled, but the Dalai Lama nursed her back to health. She was loving and got on well with the Dalai Lama's two dogs. The kitten used his Lhasa Apso, a small dog with a long, straight coat, for her furry bed. After the cat and dogs died, the Dalai Lama vowed not to have more companion animals, realizing that it was not fair to care for only a few when he was responsible for all sentient beings on earth.

On most days, the Dalai Lama participated in government and in making a better life for his people in India. The year 1969 saw the establishment of the Library of Tibetan Works and Archives. Containing more than forty thousand original Tibetan volumes, the library would publish books in both Tibetan and English. Constructed in traditional Tibetan style, the building would hold many Tibetan treasures brought to India by Tibetan refugees.

In 1970, sacred items went to a new temple. The Dalai Lama's monastery, Namgyal, was reestablished in a building close to his residence, and beside it, the School of Buddhist Dialects was founded. Through the temple, the people could celebrate Buddhist ceremonies in a proper setting; through the monastery, the continuation of Tibetan monastic life would resume; and through the school, the art of debate would be kept alive in the monastic community. The Dalai Lama was adamant about Tibetan Buddhism continuing as it had for centuries in Tibet, and soon new monasteries of Ganden, Sera, and Drepung were erected in India.

PURSUING INTERNATIONAL ATTENTION

While the exiled Tibetans tried to rebuild their lives, Tibet's cause fell further into the background, as the status of China changed in the world. In 1971, Henry Kissinger—U.S. President Richard M. Nixon's secretary of state—made a secret visit to China, paving the way for President Nixon to visit China himself. Normalization of relations between China and the United States was the result, and it had worldwide repercussions. For Tibet, it meant a cessation of aid in its fight for independence when the CIA stopped all operations in the Asian theater. The Dalai Lama saw the withdrawal as a sign that rather than fighting *for* Tibet, the United States had actually been fighting *against* Communism.

But the Dalai Lama would not be daunted. The world noticed Tibet again when he made his first trip to the West in 1973, a journey lasting six weeks and covering eleven countries.

His first stop was Rome, where he met Pope Paul VI. He compared the Vatican to the Potala, in its size and agelessness. The Swiss guards, however, seemed ludicrous to him in their brightly colored uniforms—like decorations, rather than militia. The Dalai Lama met briefly with the pope and stressed the need for increased spiritual values for all human beings, regardless of their beliefs. The pope fully agreed, and they parted cordially.

While in Scandinavia, the Dalai Lama met up with Heinrich Harrer. It pleased him to see that his old friend's sense of humor was just as down-to-earth as ever and that he was in good health. Yet Harrer's yellow hair had turned grey, a sign that the Dalai Lama was also aging. At thirty-eight, he was middle-aged by Tibetan standards and the trip exhausted him.

In the years that followed, the Dalai Lama continued to publish books, in both English and Tibetan. He had already published *The Opening of the Wisdom Eye*, his second book, in 1968, and in 1975 came *The Buddhism of Tibet and the Key to the Middle Way*. Yet with the publishing in 1976 of *Universal Responsibility and the Good Heart*, he brought one of his central philosophies into clear view. "By this I mean the responsibility that we all have for each other and for all sentient beings and also for all of Nature."[3]

In the year before this book's publication, significant events occurred to change the atmosphere in China. In January 1976, Zhou En-lai died, and in September, Mao Zedong followed him to the grave. In 1977, the president of the People's Republic of China, Li Xiannian, said that the cultural revolution had done China both good and harm, a sign that the regime of harsh policies and demands of explicit compliance was waning. China even eased attitudes toward Tibet.

In April of that year, Ngabo Ngawang Jigme, then a high-ranking member of the Chinese government, announced that China would welcome the return of the Dalai Lama to Tibet, along with those who had followed him into exile. News reports from Beijing touted the happiness Tibetans had experienced since the Chinese takeover, and called their joy "unprecedented." Mao's successor, Hua Guofeng, called for the restoration of Tibetan customs and agreed to permit Tibetans to resume dressing like Tibetans. The Dalai Lama took these as possible signs of reconciliation and hoped for China's unconditional return of his country to the Tibetan people. However, he told the Indian press that there was no hope of his returning to Tibet unless the Tibetan people were "happy and satisfied," and joked that if he returned without the country's conflicts settled, the Tibetan people might eject him.

Marking the nineteenth anniversary of the Tibetan uprising, the Dalai Lama asked China for concessions in Tibet during his annual March 10 speech in 1978. He advocated unrestricted access to Tibet for non-Tibetans and visitation rights for exiles who wanted to return to Tibet to visit their families. Although he expected his requests to be ignored, both were honored shortly after his speech, although visitations were restricted.

That same year, Deng Xiaoping became the Chinese head of state, and the Dalai Lama saw the appointment as favorable for Tibet. He saw Deng as a moderate leader, and his assessment was confirmed when dialogues opened between the two camps shortly after Deng took control.

In 1979, Gyalo Thondup came to the Dalai Lama saying that the Chinese were ready to make direct contact with him, and to prove their good faith, Gyalo Thondup had been invited to Beijing for discussions; Deng wanted Gyalo Thondup to personally relate his intentions for the visit to the Dalai Lama. The Dalai Lama advised his brother to make the trip, but said that he had no offer to make aside from explaining the real situation inside and outside Tibet. Although the Dalai Lama was still wary of the Chinese, he thought that problems could only be solved by contact and that no harm would come from hearing what China had to say.

He also sent a message to Beijing via the Chinese embassy in India proposing a fact-finding mission of delegates from the government-in-exile, who would assess the situation in Tibet and report their findings. He instructed Gyalo Thondup to pursue the same request.

DEALING WITH CHINA

Deng had indicated that negotiations on every aspect of the Tibetan situation were possible, aside from independence. Never insisting that independence was a condition of negotiations, the Dalai Lama reasoned that a peaceful solution to the Tibetan question was possible. The Dalai Lama carefully selected members for the proposed fact-finding mission. He wanted people who were familiar with both Tibet, as it had been before the Chinese takeover, and the modern world, in general. Lobsang Samten was one of those people. By this time, Lobsang Samten had renounced his monastic vows, leaving the Dalai Lama the only monk in the family. An August departure was set for the mission, pending Chinese approval.

But the Dalai Lama could not wait to see the outcome of his plan. In June, he fulfilled a commitment to visit Mongolia and the USSR. He was comfortable in Mongolia, owing to the Mongolians' close cultural ties with Tibet; however, repression was evident, as the country was under Communist control. He exchanged katas with the people there, although their katas were pale blue or slate grey, as opposed to the Tibetan white. In Moscow, he perceived the people as charming, within their strict confines of conformity to the Communist regime, and was particularly touched by the warmth he received from the Russian Orthodox community.

Gyalo Thondup returned to India from his conference in Beijing with good news—the delegation of exiles to Tibet would be accepted. The preselected members departed for China on August 2, 1979. Once in Beijing, they spent the first two weeks planning their tour of Tibet—a four-month journey that would cover the length and breadth of the country.

In the first days of their return to Tibet, people mobbed the delegates from the Tibetan government-in-exile, asking for blessings and news of the Dalai Lama, and the same enthusiasm continued throughout the journey. In Lhasa, throngs disobeyed Chinese orders to stay away from the members of the mission and filled the streets.

The mission returned to India on December 21, 1979, bringing hundreds of rolls of film, hours of recorded conversations, and more than seven thousand letters from exiles' family members. It was the first time mail had left Tibet in twenty years.

Although this raised the spirits of many, what the mission found was not encouraging. The people recounted years of starvation, public executions, and forced labor. Most of the Norbulingka's gardens were overgrown jungles, and inside its palaces, they saw mounds of shattered statuary. They brought photos of destroyed monasteries and nunneries, which had been reduced to grain stores, cattle pens, or factories,

and offered photos as proof that the Chinese were working toward eradi-
cating the Tibetan way of life.

It was true that the Tibetan economy had been strengthened and that
goods were in abundance; however, they were not commodities for average Tibetan people. The goods were intended for rich Tibetans and the
ruling Chinese. The factories produced goods that were sent directly to
China. Hydroelectric power stations had been built to light the Chinese
quarter of Lhasa, while Tibetan sectors went unwired. The delegates reported that the Chinese lived a relatively modern life in Tibet, while native Tibetans still lived in the distant past.

The Chinese had made it clear to the delegation that they wanted no
criticism from them nor from any of the exiles in India. They stated that
expatriates had no right to argue about conditions from outside Tibet, and
that if they wanted to improve the situation, it would have to be from inside the country.

Some positives did come from the delegation's visit. They had met
many young Tibetans, studying in Beijing. In talking with them, members
learned that the young people had not lost their spirits nor their love and
respect for the Dalai Lama, and that hardship in Tibet had only helped
strengthen their resolve.

Because the Dalai Lama's worst fears for Tibet had been validated, he
was more determined than ever to bring his case for Tibet before the
world. He set about planning future missions to the country with Beijing,
and sought meetings with various world leaders.

MEETING HIS PEERS AND LOSING THE PAST

In 1980, the Dalai Lama made ready for his trip to the Vatican to meet
with Pope John Paul II, and expressed his hopes for the discussion. "I look
forward with faith and hope to my meeting with the Holy Father; to an
exchange of ideas and feelings, and to his suggestions, so as to open the
door to a progressive pacification between peoples."[4] The Dalai Lama
sensed an immediate kinship with the pope, citing their similar backgrounds of humble origin. He admired the pope's broad-minded and open
attitude and found him to be a very practical man. During his trip, the
Dalai Lama also had fulfilling conversations with the archbishop of Canterbury—Dr. Robert Runcie—due to their shared spiritual and political
views, such as their belief in a spiritual person's moral obligation to help
ease the world's problems. The Dalai Lama considered his trip a big success; realizing that his spiritual counterparts held the same views of existence, he hoped they would favor Tibet's cause.

Also in 1980, Jetsun Pema traveled to Tibet with another group of fact finders. "Lhasa was now very different from the city of my childhood," she wrote. "[Our] residence, with its windows painted in blue, appeared lifeless. The following day I asked what it was used for now and was told: 'It's an inn for Chinese army officers!'"[5] Many other sites in Lhasa had changed drastically; only the Potala was recognizable to her. "Nearly all the town had been destroyed and Chinese style constructions replaced the older edifices."[6]

In Amdo, a huge crowd met the Tibetan delegation's car, and the Chinese official riding with them became so angry that he jumped out and literally beat the crowd back. In another town, she met a Muslim who told her, "You are lucky, you have something that we do not have: the Dalai Lama."[7] Aside from the determination of the Tibetan people, who overwhelmed the party with seven thousand messages for the Dalai Lama, all that she saw appalled her.

Back in India, on January 12, 1981, Diki Tsering died. Since she had been blessed with good health throughout her life, the left-side paralysis that she experienced after a stroke in 1976 was extremely difficult for her, and she had never fully recovered. The news of her death greatly saddened the Dalai Lama, especially since he had not seen her for a while. At their last meeting, he gently told her not to be afraid of death, to concentrate on sacred images, and to pray. The Dalai Lama suffered a great sense of loss when she died, but he knew they would always remain spiritually close.

This was not the only death the Dalai Lama would grieve that year. The head of his household and his cook—Bonpo—also died. Bonpo had been his surrogate mother. "Most mammals consider the creature that feeds them as the most important in their lives. That was the way I felt about Bonpo," he said. "He was my mother, my father, my entire family. When my mother died I was sad, but I didn't cry. But when Bonpo died and I looked down on his dead body, I wept."[8]

Fifteen months later, in April 1982, a three-man delegation from the Tibetan government-in-exile flew to Beijing for talks with Chinese government officials regarding the future of Tibet. They reminded China that its position was supposed to have been one of suzerainty, not overlord, and that the Seventeen-Point Agreement was testimony to the fact. They also revealed their awareness that Tibetans were miserable under the Chinese regime, regardless of the propaganda surrounding their happiness, and asked for a mutually satisfying resolution.

The Chinese government was not at all receptive to their claims and requests. They accused the Tibetan government-in-exile of using the fact-finding missions to fabricate lies. China's main objective was the return of the Dalai Lama to Tibet, and officials produced a five-clause statement of conditions for his return to his homeland. In it, they insisted that there be no more "quibbling" over the events of 1959, and required that the Dalai Lama and his followers contribute to the unity of China. They did not oblige the Dalai Lama to make his home in Tibet, but suggested that he could come and go as he wished, and stipulated a statement to the press, acknowledging the agreement.

The Dalai Lama was surprised that the Chinese would think that he was concerned with his own status, as he had always been concerned for the rights and welfare of his people alone. Believing that the highest human ability is creativity and that it can only be exercised properly in freedom, he declined to return to Tibet until his people were once again free. He hoped to make a short trip in 1984; however, that visit would never materialize.

That year, the Dalai Lama lost his brother Lobsang Samten. Only fifty-four years old, Lobsang Samten came down with influenza, which progressed to pneumonia, that turned to jaundice. He went into a coma, and after only twelve days, Lobsang Samten died.

The Dalai Lama suffered profound loss. The brothers had been close throughout their lives, but his death did not surprise the Dalai Lama. "His experiences as a member of the first fact-finding mission had affected him profoundly ... subsequently he fell into long periods of depression."[9] The Dalai Lama believes that his brother died of a broken heart.

INTERNATIONAL SUPPORT FOR TIBET

One bit of encouragement came in 1984 when ninety-one members of the United States Congress sent a letter to the Chinese president, Li Xiannian, expressing their support for direct talks between the Chinese government and the Tibetan government-in-exile. It asked President Xiannian to "grant the very reasonable and justified aspirations of His Holiness the Dalai Lama and his people every consideration."[10]

The Dalai Lama was elated that the Tibetan cause was finally receiving international recognition, and he was further encouraged by similar steps taken by other countries around the world. It seemed that a surge of interest had arisen over the Tibetan situation. To validate his opinion, in early 1987 the Dalai Lama was invited to address the Human Rights Caucus of the U.S. Congress in Washington, D.C. To prepare himself and assure further support, he began to list definite goals for the Tibetan cause, hoping that they might gain international sympathy.

During his speech, he called for Tibet to be treated as a zone of ahimsa—a state of peace and nonviolence, requiring the removal of troops. He also called for the transformation of Tibet into the world's largest park, with strict laws to enforce wildlife protection; the prohibition of nuclear power plants; the active promotion of peace and environmental protection; and the encouragement of international and regional organizations to promote and protect human rights. The Dalai Lama's thinking was that a neutral Tibet would allow both India and China a buffer zone. He saw it as good economic business for both countries, as the plan would eliminate the need for troop concentrations at the border. The ahimsa proposition was also a way to allow the nonaggressive relationship to continue between India and China, as a neutral Tibet would separate them.

China read the Dalai Lama's proposals as a declaration of independence, even though that was not at all what he intended. He merely wanted to arrive at a compromise, whereby Chinese and Tibetans could live together in peace. Since the Tibetans had nothing to offer, because everything had been taken away from them, he realized that the burden of compromise weighed more heavily on the Chinese. However, he pointed out that Tibetans would have to offer a great deal of moral strength, and that it would not be easy for his people to forget what had happened over the previous twenty-eight years.

The Dalai Lama also advocated a halt to Chinese population transfer, which began in 1959, because he saw the influx as the biggest threat to maintaining Tibetan culture. He cited statistics for the Amdo region of historical Tibet—then part of China's Qinghai province—which calculated the Chinese population at 2.5 million and the Tibetan's population at 750,000, and showed that Chinese outnumbered Tibetans in the Tibet Autonomous Region as well.

The third part of his proposition had to do with restoration of human rights in Tibet. Although by this time, some of the Tibetan monasteries had been rebuilt and New Years' celebrations—along with other religious rights—had been restored, Tibetans were still under harsh restrictions. The Dalai Lama wanted China to agree to allow Tibetans to develop culturally, intellectually, spiritually, and economically and to exercise their basic inalienable rights.

Restoration of the environment had to do with cessation of nuclear weapon production and nuclear waste dumping. The Dalai Lama learned that nuclear waste dumps in Tibet were used not only by China but also by other countries, to which China sold the privilege of dumping for hard currency. Whereas Tibet was once a wildlife sanctuary, a place where

Buddhists respected all human and animal life, parts of the area had become toxic and dangerous to all living beings. Wildlife had been destroyed—in some places completely eradicated—and there had been
irreparable damage to the forests. Due to the arid climate of Tibet, restoration would take decades, and the Dalai Lama wanted to see the ruination
of Tibet's ecological balance end.

Once again, the Chinese saw the Dalai Lama's proposals as poorly prepared, aggressive, and founded on a desire to reclaim the country and reassume control. They quickly denounced the proposals in strong terms.

Following the Chinese denunciation, demonstrations arose inside
Tibet. Lhasans turned out by the thousands to insist on freedom. However, the demonstration was short-lived. Tibetans reported that PLA soldiers fired on the crowd, killing nineteen people and wounding many
more. The Chinese, however, replied that PLA members had fired into
the air to warn the people, but that some of the rounds struck the crowd
rather than falling to the ground harmlessly.

News of this demonstration and crackdown hit world news and
brought a resurgence of interest in the Tibetan situation. In 1988, the
Dalai Lama was invited to speak before the European Parliament in Strasbourg. At this same time, several Western leaders called on China to re-
open negotiations with the Tibetan government-in-exile.

In his speech, the Dalai Lama restated his commitment to nonviolence,
but also gave this warning: "I have always urged my people not to resort to
violence in their efforts to redress their suffering. Yet I believe all people
have the moral right.... I will continue to counsel for non-violence, but
unless China forsakes the brutal methods it employs, Tibetans cannot be
responsible for a further deterioration in the situation."[11]

The Dalai Lama also used the opportunity to restate his five-point
peace plan, not advocating independence for Tibet but the right to live as
free Tibetans. He clearly stated his intentions toward China: "The Government of the People's Republic of China could remain responsible for
Tibet's foreign policy. The Government of Tibet should, however, develop
and maintain relations, through its own Foreign Affairs Bureau."[12]

The Dalai Lama also stated that he was ready to negotiate with the
Chinese, and claimed that the five-point plan, later to be called the Strasbourg Proposal, was merely a proposal. Any hard decisions were still in the
hands of the Tibetan people. Yet again, the Chinese denounced the Dalai
Lama's speech and criticized the European Parliament for allowing him to
present it.

Though the Dalai Lama was optimistic for restoration of the Tibetan
state within China, as a compromise to his true wishes for an independent

Tibet, the road to reconciliation was not even in view. Though he continued to hope for a peaceful resolution to preserve what was left of his nation and rich heritage, he knew that without talks, nothing could be accomplished, and it did not appear that the Chinese were willing to make concessions. The Dalai Lama, although frustrated, continued his fight for Tibet.

NOTES

1. Lee Feigon, *Demystifying Tibet* (Chicago: (Ivan R. Dee) Elephant Paperback 1996), p. 49.

2. Jetsun Pema, *Tibet: My Story*, p. 106.

3. Tenzin Gyatso, *Freedom in Exile*, p. 200.

4. "The Dalai Lama's Biography," Government of Tibet in Exile, www.tibet.com/DL/biography.html.

5. Jestun Pema, *Tibet: My Story*, p. 151.

6. Ibid.

7. Quoted in Jetsun Pema, *Tibet: My Story*, p. 153.

8. Quoted in Mary Craig, *Kundun*, p. 326.

9. Tenzin Gyatso, *Freedom in Exile*, p. 246.

10. United States, *Foreign Relations Authorization Act, Fiscal Years 1988 and 1989* (excerpt), Washington D.C., Government of Tibet in Exile, www.tibet.com/Resolution/us8889.html.

11. "Address to Members of the European Parliament by His Holiness the Dalai Lama" (Strasbourg, 15 June 1988). The Government of Tibet in Exile. www.tibet.com/Proposal/strasbourg.html.

12. Ibid.

Chapter 11

AN IMPROVED POSITION
IN THE WORLD

By the end of the 1980s the Dalai Lama had become more than a religious icon and the political leader of a distressed nation; he had become a celebrity. His international profile upset the Chinese government, for not only was he a thorn in their side, but also his popularity served to embarrass them before the world.

China's relations with the United States had been strained since the Communist takeover, yet the ease in tensions that began with Richard Nixon's historic visit in 1972 culminated in formal recognition by the United States in 1979. The People's Republic of China could not allow its new status in the world to be jeopardized by continued criticism from the Tibetan sector.

Still, China would not accept an independent Tibet. Officials continually refuted the argument that Tibet had ever been independent, and in no way saw their actions in 1950 and beyond as anything other than dealing with civil uprising. The Dalai Lama's Strasbourg Proposal was clearly unacceptable to the Chinese.

They were, however, anxious to make the situation go away. Although they had rejected the Dalai Lama's proposal, they did not reject the idea of further talks. On September 23, 1988, they delivered a formal response to the Dalai Lama's plan: "We welcome the Dalai Lama to have talks with the Central Government at any time.... But there is one condition, that is, no foreigners should be involved. We are ready to designate one official with certain rank to have direct dialogue with the Dalai Lama."[1]

The Chinese also stipulated that two points needed clarification. They declared that they had never recognized the Dalai Lama's cabinet and would not accept any delegations designated by the government-in-exile. Neither would they consider any talks based upon the Dalai Lama's Strasbourg plan, as it did not clearly relinquish the Tibetan claim to independence. China urged the Dalai Lama to give up all thoughts of sovereignty for Tibet and to place himself in the great bosom of the motherland.

Already realizing that the Chinese would reject the offer, the Tibetan government-in-exile quickly announced that talks would begin in Geneva in January of 1989, and provided names for a team of negotiators, including a Dutch lawyer. The Dalai Lama did not plan to take part in the discussions. The Chinese were furious at the blatant negation of their offer, and saw the Dalai Lama's announcement of the meeting as a complete breech of diplomacy. Obviously, the Dalai Lama and his advisors had thrown the ball back into their court.

The Chinese embassy in New Delhi immediately phoned Gyalo Thondup and accused the Tibetans of insincerity, saying that the Dalai Lama should have discussed the venue and time of the meeting with them before making public statements to the press. No meeting ever took place, and their decade-long dialogues were curtailed. Clearly, neither side was willing to make concessions.

ABOVE ALL, COMPASSION

In Tibet, the situation remained tenuous, as many demonstrations had taken place in the months preceding January 1989. On the twenty-eighth of that month, the Panchen Lama died at his home in Shigatse—another blow to the Chinese, as he had been instrumental in helping to quell Tibet's anger. On March 5, the largest demonstration since 1959 took place in Lhasa, and it lasted three days. Up to 750 Tibetans were killed in the rioting that overwhelmed the city, and on March 8, the Chinese imposed martial law.

None of this, however, would sway the Dalai Lama from his spiritual beliefs. He wanted Tibetans to understand their enemies. "For it is under the greatest adversity that there exists the greatest potential for doing good, both for oneself and others."[2]

This compassion, even for his enemies, won the Dalai Lama the Nobel Peace Prize in 1989. In his acceptance speech in Stockholm, he further demonstrated his compassion: "I pray for all of us, oppressor and friend, that together we succeed in building a better world through human understanding and love, and that in doing so we may reduce the pain and suffering of all sentient beings."[3] He furthered his stance in his Nobel Prize lecture by saying, "I am always reminded that we are all basically alike: we are all human beings. Maybe we have different clothes, our skin is of a different colour, or we speak different languages. That is on the surface. But basically, we are the same human beings. That is what binds us to each other. That is what makes it possible for us to understand each other and to develop friendship and closeness."[4]

More than a mere accolade for the Dalai Lama, the Nobel Peace Prize gave him increased credibility within international political circles, causing China to suffer a major diplomatic humiliation. From then on, the Dalai Lama would be seen as an emissary of peace living in exile, while his downtrodden people lived under the thumb of China. It was good public relations, and the Dalai Lama used his edge wisely.

In December of 1989, the Dalai Lama carried this sphere of compassion into Germany, and was present when the Berlin Wall was toppled. While he stood looking at the once formidable guard tower, an old woman came up to him and handed him a red candle. A crowd pressed around the Dalai Lama, who lit the candle and accepted their hands touching his, as he held the flickering flame. He prayed that the light of compassion and enlightenment would fill the world, and said it was a moment he would always remember.

May 11, 1990, brought reforms to the Tibetan government-in-exile that would evoke anxiety over changes in tradition as well as hope for the future. On this day, the Dalai Lama offered true democracy to exiled Tibetans by dissolving his personally appointed cabinet, along with the Tenth Assembly of Tibetan People's Deputies—the Tibetan parliament. The Dalai Lama spoke to his people, saying, "From now on, the people's decision will be final. I feel that the Dalai Lama should have no role here. The future assembly will be entrusted with the power of appointing the [ministers]."[5] The Dalai Lama also outlined his proposals for granting women greater representation, for instituting two houses in the legislature, and for establishing a judicial tribunal to fully service the needs of a democratic society.

In that same year, the exiles in India, along with Tibetans living in thirty-three other countries, elected the forty-six members of the Eleventh Tibetan Parliament on a one-person, one-vote basis. The parliament then elected the members of the cabinet, and the new constitution resulting from this reform was titled The Charter of Tibetans in Exile. The new constitution not only provided for basic freedoms for its people but also outlined the form of the new Tibetan government-in-exile.

Another big step forward came in April 1991 when the Dalai Lama met with U.S. President George Bush—the first meeting between a U.S. president and a Dalai Lama in history. During the conversation, a discussion of "new world order," based on a concept of global unity and cooperation, arose. The Dalai Lama said to President Bush, "A New World Order with compassion is very good. I'm not so sure about a New World Order without compassion."[6] Bush's public statements indicating advocacy for a more democratic China encouraged the Dalai Lama, and he expressed his hope that the United States would continue to press for an end to China's repressive policies.

CHINA'S PRESSURE POINT

Although the Tibetans in exile saw increasing support from the West, their negotiations with China were at a standstill. Beijing was not interested in any proposal that would release Tibet from the same laws and consideration that applied to any other part of China, while the Tibetans pushed for civil autonomy and cultural and religious freedom. Tibetan concessions to Chinese international representation was not enough, and the Tibetans took the next step in September 1991, when the newly elected chairman of the cabinet, Gyalo Thondup, said:

His Holiness the Dalai Lama made it very clear in his statement on 10th March this year that because of the closed and negative attitude of the present Chinese leadership, he felt that his personal commitment to the ideas expressed in the Strasbourg proposal had become ineffectual, and that if there were no new initiatives from the Chinese, he would consider himself free of any obligation to the proposals he had made in his Strasbourg address.[7]

He went on to say that the Dalai Lama was still firmly committed to his path of nonviolence and that he hoped to find an answer for Tibet through negotiations and greater understanding.

The United States again stepped in on the side of Tibet on November 26, 1992, when the U.S. House of Representatives voted in favor of conditioning China's most-favored-nation status, which allows China to trade with the United States at the lowest tariff rate available. This privilege was granted to China in 1980 with the stipulation that it be reviewed each year before renewal, as opposed to other countries that attain and hold this status in perpetuity. The 1992 House action stated that China's status would be revoked as of July 1993 unless President Bill Clinton presented a report to Congress stating that China had complied with several requirements, one being the accounting for and releasing of prisoners incarcerated for the nonviolent expression of their religious beliefs.

Congress also expected China to verify progress in the area of human rights, especially in the prevention of gross violations in Tibet.

When President Clinton issued Executive Order 12850 on May 28, 1993, it included the proviso that the secretary of state would determine whether China had made significant progress in the areas Congress had insisted on, and included the condition for "protecting Tibet's distinctive religious and cultural heritage."[8] For the first time, China's economic well-being was tied to issues in Tibet.

Soon after, Clinton invited the Dalai Lama to meet with him and Vice President Al Gore at the White House in 1994. Bill Clinton would, in fact, meet with the Dalai Lama five times, each time on the pretense of "dropping in" while he met with lesser officials. The United States did not want to endanger relations with China or its allies by treating the Dalai Lama as though he were the Tibetan head of state. During the discussions, the Dalai Lama urged U.S. leaders to hold talks with Beijing and encourage the world's most populous nation to embrace democracy. He told reporters, "The free world, and especially the United States ... [has] great responsibility to bring democracy into China."[9]

American sentiment for the Tibetan issue and the Dalai Lama has been mixed. Whereas empathies lie with the Tibetans now under Chinese rule, business interests are quick to avoid trouble with China. Concerning these visits, China's *People's Daily* reported, "He has long sat outside China and has gone to the corners of the world in an effort to split Tibet from China. There is not one thing religiously pure about him. The political words and actions of the Dalai Lama have long ago torn to shreds his religious mantle."[10]

Yet amid Chinese protests, the United States government recognizes Tibet as an autonomous region under Chinese rule and the Dalai Lama as its political and spiritual leader. The Dalai Lama sees Americans as friends. "Because in the past both houses [of Congress] have shown very good support. So this is, I think, one of the great sources of hope and also encouragement to me."[11]

The Dalai Lama, however, had more than China to contend with, and his international status did nothing to aid the sentiments growing in Dharamsala between members of the Gaddi tribe—indigenous to Dharamsala—and the Tibetan exiles. On April 23, 1994, rioting broke out in the streets over the killing of a Gaddi tribe member by a Tibetan. Scores of Indians demanded that the Tibetans leave Dharamsala and marched through the streets, shouting slogans against the Dalai Lama.

When the melee occurred, the Dalai Lama was in the United States. Immediately upon his return, he issued a statement expressing his great remorse over the entire incident: "The incident was most unfortunate and I was deeply pained to learn about it."[12] He expressed remorse over the damage done to the Tibetan settlement and promised to take immediate action on issues directly relating to Tibetans. The Dalai Lama also offered to leave Dharamsala and petitioned the Indian government to move his headquarters to Bangalore in the southern tip of India, hoping to reduce the concentration of Tibetans in one area as well as the number of visitors who came to visit the town from around the world on his behalf.

Upon hearing of his request, the Indian community of Dharamsala sent several delegations asking the Dalai Lama to stay. The groups included members of the Gaddi tribe, the Lions Club, and several other business or-ganizations, as well as headmen of villages surrounding Dharamsala. The members also promised to stop politicians from exploiting incidents be-tween Tibetan and Indian factions to create animosity in the community. Due to this overwhelming response, the Dalai Lama withdrew his request to move the government-in-exile south, and remained in Dharamsala.

THE PANCHEN LAMA DISPUTE

The year following the uprising saw another kind of conflict for the Dalai Lama. Since 1989, when the Panchen Lama died, the Dalai Lama and his followers had searched for his reincarnation; however, they did so with no mandate from China. At the start, the Dalai Lama proposed to send a ten-member delegation of religious personnel to Tibet in order to perform the Kalachakra ceremony for the departed Panchen Lama and to begin their search. Chinese authorities rejected his request, saying that they wanted no "outsiders" involved in the process. To all Tibetan Bud-dhists, this was unthinkable. No Panchen Lama could possibly be en-throned without the approval of the Dalai Lama.

In 1991, the Dalai Lama asked the Chinese government for high lamas to be permitted to observe prophetic visions in Lake Lhamo Lhatso, as Reting Rinpoché had done in his search for the Dalai Lama. Three months later, Chinese officials responded that there was no need for out-side interference.

A member of Tashilhunpho Monastery, the seat of the Panchen Lama, was selected by the Chinese to find the Panchen Lama's reincarnation in 1993. The following month, the government-in-exile invited the repre-sentative to India to discuss his search; the exiles never received a re-sponse.

In 1995, disregarding the Chinese government, the Dalai Lama pub-licly proclaimed the Eleventh Panchen Lama—a six-year-old boy, born four months after the Tenth Panchen Lama's death to a family of semino-madic people in the northeastern region of Tibet. The Dalai Lama said, "I have given him the name Tenzin Gedhun Yeshe Thrinley Phuntsog Pal Sangpo, and have composed a long-life prayer titled 'Spontaneous Fulfill-ment of the Wishes.'"[13] He saw the choice of a new Panchen Lama as a re-ligious matter rather than a political one, and expressed his hope that the Chinese government would be cooperative.

The Chinese were not only unsupportive of the decision but infuriated by the Dalai Lama's independent actions and refused his choice. China stood on the old custom of lot drawing via the "golden urn," and said that all reincarnations had to be approved by China's central government. In fact, they claimed that all Dalai Lamas and Panchen Lamas had been cho-sen and approved in this manner since 1792. A Chinese news agency re-port from 1995 quoted a spokesman from the Chinese Bureau of Religious Affairs as saying, "In disregard of fixed historical convention, undermin-ing religious rituals, disrupting the normal searching process, and negating the supreme authority of the Central Government in the matter concern-ing the reincarnation of Panchen Lama, Dalai Lama went so far as openly announcing a reincarnated child for Panchen Lama abroad. This is totally illegal and invalid."[14]

China also saw the Dalai Lama's actions as further indication of his de-sire for Tibetan independence. "This fully demonstrates the political plot of the Dalai clique in its continuous splittist activities by making use of Panchen Lama's reincarnation after repeated failures in its acts abroad aimed at splitting the motherland," the religious-affairs spokesman told Reuters News Agency.[15]

The Dalai Lama's first strike angered China. Officials had hoped to an-nounce the new Panchen Lama as an indication of religious freedom in Tibet, and were waiting to declare their choice at the thirtieth anniver-sary of the establishment of the Tibet Autonomous Region. Though the Dalai Lama had won the public-relations upper hand, his government put themselves at odds with the Chinese once again, hindering any negotia-tions over the state of Tibet.

When the United States backed the Dalai Lama's choice for Panchen Lama, the situation only worsened. A State Department spokesman said, "We are concerned that disagreements or controversies about the reincar-nation of the Panchen Lama might raise additional doubts about the Chi-nese Government's commitment to respecting the religious beliefs and practices of Tibetan Buddhists."[16] The Chinese took decisive action.

By the end of May, both the man chosen by the Chinese to find the Panchen Lama and the Dalai Lama's candidate were sequestered in Beijing with no further word. The Chinese government suspected its representative of collaborating with the Dalai Lama on the announcement of the Panchen Lama's discovery through secret channels. In Lhasa, meetings with government officials and high-ranking lamas were required to denounce the Dalai Lama's statement, although Tibetans expressed their refusal to accept any candidate not validated by the Dalai Lama himself.

On June 16, the Dalai Lama accused Chinese authorities of kidnapping the Panchen Lama and his parents, although Chinese officials denied the charges. In October, they declared their intention to find a replacement for the Dalai Lama's choice, which they did the following month, when another six-year-old Tibetan boy was chosen by the golden urn method. The United States Senate was quick to react to the Chinese decision and unanimously adopted a resolution urging the Chinese government to accept the Dalai Lama's choice.

GAINING SUPPORT AND LOSING THE BATTLE

International murmurs over Chinese interference in Tibetan Buddhist religious rituals only served to heighten Chinese animosity toward the Dalai Lama. On April 5, 1996, *Xizang Ribao*, a local Tibetan newspaper with a Chinese slant—reported: "Lately, the Dalai splittist clique has stepped up its splittist, infiltrative and rebellious instigative activities in Tibet. It has colluded with domestic forces and forces outside the country in rampantly carrying out reactionary propaganda in Tibet, especially in religious activities centers, thereby disrupting the stability of Tibet's religious circles and religious activities centers."[17] The article also cited Chinese documents that called for the banning of the Dalai Lama's portrait in temples, and said that the Dalai Lama could no longer bring happiness to his people. The Inter Press Service, a global news agency, also reported that plainclothes police officers went around ordering hotels and restaurants in Lhasa to remove all images of the exiled leader. This followed the July 1994 ban of Dalai Lama photographs from all governmental offices, and was a bold attempt at trying to remove the Dalai Lama from his dominant position in the Tibetan religion. Unrest spread throughout Lhasa. Tibetans would not be so easily swayed from their worship of the Dalai Lama.

"Really," the Dalai Lama told *Asiaweek* at the time, "if the Chinese had treated Tibetans like real brothers, then the Dalai Lama might not be so popular. All credit goes to the Chinese."[18]

By 1996, the Dalai Lama's fame had spread worldwide, and many celebrities—such as American actors Richard Gere, Tim Robbins, Steven

Seagal, Susan Sarandon, and Meg Ryan, as well as Oliver Stone—had taken a personal interest in him. In 1997, two films were released, outlining the Dalai Lama's life. *Kundun* focused on the Dalai Lama's life from his discovery through his escape into India. *Seven Years in Tibet*, based on Heinrich Harrer's experiences in the Forbidden City, starred actor Brad Pitt and was the more financially successful of the two films.

Screenwriter Melissa Mathison, who penned *Kundun*, was quoted as saying, "He asked me if people would want to see his story.... would people care? He saw it as a great opportunity for people to learn about Tibet and to preserve part of history. He felt he'd have a piece of history to give his people."[19]

In 1998, the Dalai Lama faced serious opposition to his nonviolent "middle-way" position on Tibetan autonomy. A group of exiles staged a "fast unto death" hunger strike in the early part of the year. When six were taken to a New Delhi hospital, another activist set fire to himself in protest. This led the Dalai Lama to admit, "For many years, I'd been able to persuade the Tibetan people to eschew violence in our freedom struggle."[20] Tibetan violence had begun. Although he had predicted it in his speech to the European Parliament in 1988, he was discouraged.

Although the Dalai Lama pressed harder for talks with the Chinese central government, China's closed door against Tibetan independence was firmly shut. "The Dalai Lama suspended his contact with the central government when he thought the international situation was in his favour and now demands negotiations when he thinks the situation is moving against him," a *Xinhua* report of March 1998 read. The report based its hard line on the Dalai Lama's rejection of three conditions for talks, laid down by then Chinese President Jiang Zemin in 1989: acceptance of Tibet as an inalienable part of China, abandonment of Tibetan independence, and abatement of all activities designed to "split the motherland."

At that same time the reins of Chinese government were passing to a new leader, Prime Minister Zhu Rongji, and the Dalai Lama was certain he was more open-minded than the previous regime. Soon after the new administration took over, however, the Dalai Lama found that nothing had changed; a Chinese Foreign Ministry spokesperson told the press: "The high degree of autonomy advocated by the Dalai Lama is in essence a two-step strategy for Tibetan independence. Its purpose is to fool international opinion."[21]

Yet the Dalai Lama opted to maintain hope, and said, "Judging by the overall changing situation in China, I think eventually some kind of understanding will come."[22]

Tibetan dissidents, however, took a dim view of his philosophy. They thought that the Dalai Lama's stance had stagnated the drive for Tibetan independence, and they were losing patience with the nonviolent approach. The hunger strikes and act of self-immolation in the early part of the year put the Dalai Lama into a quandary, which he freely admitted. However, going against his philosophy of nonviolence would be counter to his beliefs. He realized that his middle way was not as effective as it needed to be to attain freedom for Tibet, but saw no other road except communication with China.

MORE PROMISES, LESS PROGRESS

In June of that year, the Dalai Lama admitted to having informal contacts with Beijing through various private communication channels. Chinese President Jiang Zemin openly confirmed this, and in October, a report was released by the French press, claiming that the Dalai Lama was preparing a statement on the political status of Tibet, which he intended to present at a meeting with Jiang Zemin. The Dalai Lama hoped to meet the Chinese president as a monk rather than a politician. The Tibetans guessed it was their best prospect for a breakthrough since 1988.

Hopes were soon dashed, however, when China replied to the Dalai Lama's request by accusing him of insincerity and of ignoring official channels of communication. They held their position that talks would not happen until the Dalai Lama made public statements acknowledging China's sovereignty over Tibet. By November, all hopes for talks were abandoned.

Tibet continues to be part of China, and the Dalai Lama and the Chinese government continue to flirt with the idea of talks. The Dalai Lama stands on his demand for autonomy for Tibet rather than independence, and is still hopeful that communication will return his homeland to his people. The Chinese say that he is not a simple monk but a politician hiding under his Buddhist robe, intent on splitting the motherland.

The Dalai Lama continues to visit countries around the world, urging world leaders to open China's great wall of resistance just a crack, so that he may state his case and make headway in the autonomy he desires for the Tibetan people.

He has also taken steps so that the Tibetan government-in-exile will run smoothly without him. For the first time, the chairman of the cabinet was elected by the people rather than appointed by the Dalai Lama, which had been done for centuries. "The Tibet struggle is not for the Dalai Lama or for any individual . . . . Our struggle is for our nation. Individuals may go. The struggle will remain. Sooner or later, I will die. At the time of my death, there may be some setback. Our organization should carry the work as if there is no Dalai Lama."[23]

NOTES

1. Quoted in Tsering Shakya, *The Dragon in the Land of Snows*, pp. 425–426.

2. Tenzin Gyatso, *Freedom in Exile*, p. 261.

3. "His Holiness the Dalai Lama's Acceptance Speech for the Nobel Prize for Peace" (University of Aula, Oslo, 10 December 1989.

4. (Tenzin Gyatso), "Nobel Lecture," 11 December 1989.

5. Tibetan Parliamentary and Policy Research Centre, "Tibet's Parliament in Exile," TibetNet, www.tibet.net/eng/atpd/progress (1999).

6. His Holiness the Fourteenth Dalai Lama, *Dimensions of Spirituality* (Somerville, MA: Wisdom Publications, 1995), www.wisdompubs.org/booklets/dimensions.html

7. International Committee of Lawyers for Tibet, "Strasbourg Proposal No Longer Binding (1991)," 2 September 1991, www.tibetjustice.org/materials/tibet/tibet5.html.

8. William J. Clinton, Executive Order, EO12850, 28 May 1993.

9. Sarah Jackson-Han, "Dalai Lama Urges US to Press China toward Democracy," *l'Agence France-Presse*, 12 September 1995.

10. Quoted in "People's Daily Blasts Clinton's Visit with Dalai Lama," Kyodo News International, 21 September 1995.

11. "U.S.-China Relations Stressed. Dalai Lama: For Tibet's Sake, Washington, Beijing Must Talk," *Washington Times*, 16 September 1995.

12. Canada Tibet Committee, World Tibet Network, "Statement of His Holiness the Dalai Lama," 3 May 1994, www.tibet.ca/wtnarchive/1994/5/3–2_1.html.

13. Clarence Fernandez, "Dalai Lama Proclaims Tibet's 11th Panchen Lama," *Reuters*, May 1995.

14. "Dalai Lama's Confirmation of Reincarnation Invalid," *Xinhua*, 17 May 1995.

15. Jane MacCartney, "China Rejects Dalai Lama on Monk Reincarnation," *Reuters*, 17 May 1995.

16. Quoted at Canada Tibet Committee, World Tibet Network, "State Department Spokesman Response to Question on Chinese Rejection of New Panchen Lama," 17 May 1995.

17. Feng Yongfeng, "Tibet Bans Pictures of Dalai Lama," *Xizang Ribao*, Lhasa, 5 April 1996, p. 1.

18. Quoted in John Christensen, "Dalai Lama: Man of Peace Takes Center Stage," *CNN Interactive*, 1999, www.cnn.com/SPECIALS/1999china.50/inside.china/profiles/dalai.lama/.

19. Natasha Stoynoff, "Spiritual Homecoming," *Toronto Sun*, 4 January 1998, www.acmi.canoe.ca/JamMoviesFeaturesK/kundun_1.html.

20. "Dalai Lama Admits Failure," *Associated Press*, 29 April 1998.

21. "China Lays Down Hard Line on Tibet's Dalai Lama," *Reuters*, 30 April 1998.

22. "Dalai Lama Wants China Dialogue," *Associated Press*, 30 April 1998.

23. Pushp Saraf, "Dalai Lama Plans a Future without Him," *Border Affairs*, October–December 2001.

Chapter 12

THE DALAI LAMA'S DAILY LIFE

Although the Dalai Lama's life revolves around his struggle for a free Tibet, when in Dharamsala, he has a daily life, just as anyone else. He has never thought of himself as a god-king, only as a simple monk who prefers a simple life.

The largest part of the Dalai Lama's day is spent in meditation. He rises at 4 A.M. and starts his day by reciting mantras—words that help to still the mind. Afterward, he takes Tibetan herbal medication, rather like vitamins, with a glass of hot water, then makes prostrations to the Buddha. After his daily grooming, he walks until breakfast, which he has around 5:15 A.M. During his meal, he reads Buddhist scripture.

After breakfast, the Dalai Lama meditates until 8:00 A.M., pausing only to listen to the news on BBC (British Broadcasting Company) radio. About his meditations, he said, "In this type of meditation, one uses reasoning. Reasoning can enhance positive states of mind and overcome the attitudes, thoughts and emotions that lead to suffering and dissatisfaction."[1]

For the rest of the morning, he studies Buddhist philosophy. At noon, he shifts to reading official papers or newspapers until lunch, a half-hour later, when he switches back to Buddhist scripture.

Work for the Tibetan government-in-exile begins at 1 P.M. when the Dalai Lama deals with administrative matters and holds audiences. At 5 P.M., he returns to his quarters and begins another short period of prayer and meditation. He then watches television until tea at 6 P.M., and especially likes to watch reruns of M*A*S*H. After tea, which Americans might consider dinner, he again reads scripture and prays until 8:30 or 9:00, when he retires and falls into a very sound sleep.

Variations in his routine include participating in ceremonies, teaching, writing, or traveling. But even when traveling, he tries to complete at least five hours of prayer, meditation, and study each day. One of his favorite prayers is:

For as long as space endures
And for as long as living beings remain,
Until then may I too abide
To dispel the misery of the world.[2]

The Private Office handles all of the Dalai Lama's income and expenses. He rarely has contact with money, although he is paid a stipend by the Indian government of about twenty rupees a day—equal to about forty-two cents American—which is supposed to cover his food and clothing. However, when he received 300,000 Swedish crowns for winning the Nobel Prize in 1989, worth at that time around $480,000, he was personally able to direct how the money was spent.

TRAVEL IMPRESSIONS

In directing his political influence, the Dalai Lama has traveled to many countries around the world. He made his first journey outside India in 1967, when he traveled first to Japan and then to Thailand. He says that in Tokyo, he found signs of humans' better nature. He was amazed by the tidiness, taken to a degree he had never seen before. He felt that the food was also orderly and exquisitely presented, but that the presentation on the plate might supersede the chef's desire to accommodate taste. The constant flow of traffic was also surprising to the Dalai Lama, as well as the fact that the technological and material advancements of Japan had not sublimated their desire to preserve Japanese culture and ethics. For the first time, he saw the potential of modern technology.

In Thailand, he found the people most amiable, yet he was disappointed in the Thai need to be formal in respect to him. He found that acknowledgment of deference to him was taboo, and it was hard for him to get used to. Normally, he extends his hand or offers a kata to those who venerate him and says that regardless of Thai customs, his hand sometimes had a mind of its own.

He also found the heat in Thailand oppressive, even more severe than that of southern India. Plus, the mosquitoes there made sleeping very difficult. Yet he found some senior Buddhist monks there who delighted him in their knowledge of religion, and discovered that many Tibetan

Buddhist practices were similar to those in Thailand. He then realized that Tibetan Buddhism is a comprehensive form of his faith.

During his 1973 trip to Europe and Scandinavia, the Dalai Lama stopped in Switzerland to visit the two hundred Tibetan children who had been adopted by Swiss families. He was pleased to see that the Swiss people had treated them with loving kindness and that they were happy and well-adjusted.

He also spent ten days in the United Kingdom, and found validation for his belief that England had the closest ties with Tibet. He ran into older people there who were able to speak Tibetan, due to their being stationed in India while England ruled the country. He also met up with Hugh Richardson, former head of the British Trade Mission and author of several books about Tibet. These old friends aside, the Dalai Lama formed an opinion of the British people as very reserved and formal.

The Dalai Lama was most anxious to see the United States, which he considered the wealthiest and most open nation on earth. He was finally able to arrange a trip in 1979.

Upon arriving in New York, he was taken by the people, who seemed open, relaxed, and liberated. Yet he was amazed at the dirtiness of some parts of the city, and was appalled by the plight of the homeless, sleeping in doorways and pandering on the streets. He was taken aback by their numbers, considering the affluence of the nation where they lived. But most upsetting to him was the population's general lack of knowledge about the situation in Tibet. He concluded that in some ways, the American political system did not stand up to its own philosophies.

Nevertheless, he still enjoyed the visit, and found enormous expressions of support, especially among student audiences. The Dalai Lama's English was still not as good as it might have been, but the kindness with which everyone approached him helped him to overcome his reluctance to speak in public.

The Dalai Lama has been back to these countries many times since his initial visits. Early on, he learned that people are the same all over the world, with just a few minor distinctions. He sees everyone as seeking happiness, affection, friendship, and understanding, and understands that he can relate to all people in the world on this basis.

UNIVERSAL RESPONSIBILITY

This ability to share the world with all beings confirmed the Dalai Lama's belief in the philosophy of universal responsibility. Because we are all brothers and sisters, he believes that it is important for us to take responsibility for each other and for all things in nature. He feels that the sooner people begin to realize this, the more likely we will be to advance as human beings. He also believes that each of us is universally responsible to assure human rights for all. In 1973, he told the United Nations World Conference on Human Rights, "The question of human rights is so fundamentally important that there should be no difference of views on this. We must therefore insist on a global consensus not only on the need to respect human rights world wide but more importantly on the definition of these rights."[3] He continues to work toward a consensus, not only for Tibetans but for all suffering people of the world. He sees it as part of his duty as both a man and a spiritual person.

Although the Dalai Lama's life revolves around his faith, he is strongly against proselytizing. He himself takes knowledge from all spiritual disciplines, and encourages those interested in the Buddhist way of life to integrate the Buddhist philosophies into their lives without denouncing their own religion. He sees sectarianism as poison.

The recent surge of interest in Buddhism in the West concerns him because he thinks that many westerners do not understand what Buddhism is really about. He discourages migration to India or Tibet, and said, "If you're chasing understanding all over the world, you're not getting it."[4]

The Dalai Lama tries to live his life in what he calls the bodhisattva ideal, or the desire to be compassionate with abundant wisdom. Four root vows govern his life: not to kill, steal, or lie, and to be celibate. If a monk breaks any of these vows, he is no longer a monk.

Celibacy is often viewed by secular people as archaic and unnecessary, yet the Dalai Lama sees his vow of celibacy not as suppressing his sexual desires but as filling them with alternate means. He fully accepts the desires and transcends them with reason. To the Dalai Lama, sexual desire is not an intellectual decision, and its fulfillment is only temporary.

Nonviolence is another central tenet of the Dalai Lama's belief system, and he continues to promote this ethic in his country's struggle for independence. Yet terrorism is something the Dalai Lama finds difficult to accept and to deal with. After the World Trade Center and Pentagon bombings of September 11, 2001, he sent a letter to U.S. President George W. Bush, expressing the condolences of the Tibetan people and himself, and questioning whether a return of violence was the solution: "It may seem presumptuous on my part, but I personally believe we need to think seriously whether a violent action is the right thing to do and in the greater interest of the nation and people in the long run. I believe violence will only increase the cycle of violence. But how do we deal with hatred and anger, which are often the root causes of such senseless violence?"[5] He ended by saying that he was sure the president would make the right decision.

After the war in Afghanistan began, the Dalai Lama took a stance that surprised many people. In a press conference following a speech before the European Parliament in October 2001, he said: "I think the American side is ... taking maximum precautions about the civilian casualties."[6] He viewed this as a sign of greater civilization.

PERSONAL RELATIONSHIPS

The Dalai Lama has met and enjoyed many people in his life. One of the first celebrities he met was writer and poet Father Thomas Merton in 1968. In a letter to his abbott after the meeting, Father Merton wrote that he had met few people with whom he clicked so well. The Dalai Lama sensed the same camaraderie. He was struck by Merton's humbleness and deep spirituality, and says it was Merton who introduced him to the real meaning of "Christian." In 1996, he visited Merton's grave for the first time and said, "Now our spirits are one; I am at peace."[7]

The Dalai Lama also has a great respect for the memory of Mother Theresa, whom he saw as absolutely humble, and suggests that from a Buddhist standpoint, she would be considered a bodhisattva. Upon her death, he stated, "She was a living example of the human capacity to generate infinite love, compassion, and altruism,"[8] and he saw her as an inspiring example of a deeply spiritual life.

When the Dalai Lama met former British Prime Minister Edward Heath, he had mixed feelings. He felt as if Heath, like Nehru before him, only half listened to what the Dalai Lama had to say, yet they had several frank discussions on the Tibetan situation. Mr. Heath felt that China needed to succeed, especially in the area of agriculture, and as a recent visitor to Tibet, he told the Dalai Lama that many changes had taken place there. He felt that sentiment for the Dalai Lama was waning, especially among young people.

In a 1995 debate before the House of Commons, Sir Edward Heath stated: "It may well be that the great majority of people in Tibet today do not want the Dalai Lama back, but if he wants to return, he was told ten years ago that he could go back as the spiritual leader of all his flock in Tibet. In that respect, he cannot complain, but he has never gone back. He has never gone to Beijing to discuss it further."[9] He was not the only prime minister to feel this way. Margaret Thatcher refused to meet with the Dalai Lama at all, and said that "the interests of Hong Kong have to be taken into account."[10]

However, the president of the Czech Republic, Vaclav Havel, invited the Dalai Lama to meet with him as one of the first foreign dignitaries to visit the newly liberated country. While there, he led a mediation session for the newly elected president and his ministers. The Dalai Lama felt greatly honored to have been one of his first guests and found Havel to be gentle, honest, humble, and very funny. He has been back to the Czech Republic many times since then.

He also considers former U.S. President Bill Clinton to be an old friend. Clinton has always been a strong supporter of Tibet, and during a news conference with President Jiang Zemin in Beijing on June 27, 1998, Clinton said, "And let me say something that will perhaps be unpopular with everyone. I have spent time with the Dalai Lama. I believe him to be an honest man. And I believe if he had a conversation with President Jiang, they would like each other very much."[11]

HONOR AND THE FUTURE

The Dalai Lama's affability and hard work on behalf of his people have earned him many awards over the years, beginning with the bestowal of a doctor of letters degree from Benares Hindu University in India in 1957. Aside from the Nobel Prize, other awards include the Albert Schweitzer Humanitarian Award (1987), the Raoul Wallenberg Human Rights Award (1989), a doctorate in human arts and letters from Columbia University (1994), and a Lifetime Achievement Award from Hadassah Women's Zionist Organization in Jerusalem (1999). U.S. Congressman Tom Lantos presented the Dalai Lama with the Wallenberg award and said, "His Holiness the Dalai Lama's courageous struggle has distinguished him as a leading proponent of human rights and world peace."[12] In 2003, he is to receive the Alexandra Tolstoy Humanitarian Award.

Regardless of the famous people he has met, the awards he has received, and his own "celebrity" status, the Dalai Lama still sees himself as a humble monk, and definitely not as the "living Buddha." However, he still lives a life of limitations. A majority of Tibetan people refuse to see him as anything but a god, and even fluent English speakers are too intimidated to translate for him; his staff is inexperienced in the countryside of a country not his own; and no matter how hard he tries to promote democracy, the Tibetan community still reveres the Dalai Lama and sees him as an autocrat.

Unlike what one might expect, the Dalia Lama is not ethereal in appearance. He is tall, but the sixty-seven-year-old monk, who was once heavy-set, is now thinner. He keeps his head shorn close to the scalp and gray stubble often shows at his temples. A large pair of wire-rimmed glasses, which were once considered un-Tibetan and became acceptable only when the Dalai Lama began wearing them, are perched on his ears, which stand out a little from his head. He always wears his monk's robes of crimson and yellow, and one may see heavy work boots peeping out from under the hem.

Still, he is as pragmatic as the shoes he chooses. Referring to his public persona, writer Chris Colin described his as "Ghandi meets P.T. Barnum, minus the elephants."[13] There is always a crowd, always an audience, but never a disappointment. The Dalai Lama's charisma is boundless, and he makes friends wherever he goes.

He is also constantly trying to learn the truth about our collective existence and has an intense fascination with science. While he claims to be inept with computers, he views the Internet as a tool for human interaction and a metaphor for his philosophy of universal responsibility. "I really admire these great scientists," he said. "I'm really keen to learn, especially quantum physics. But then, it seems I understand something but as soon as the lesson is finished there's nothing left in my mind."[14]

He is also interested in learning cosmology and particle physics, and has spoken with neurosurgeons, mathematicians, and astronomers in his quest to find the place where Eastern mysticism coincides with Western science. And he believes in aliens: "Sentient forms of life, similar to human beings, do exist on other planets. Not necessarily in our solar system, but beyond. This, I believe."[15]

When at home, the Dalai Lama is still an avid gardener and uses a stationary bicycle, along with brisk walking, for his daily exercise. He wants nothing more than to enjoy these pursuits and to drop out of politics altogether. In fact, he says that if Tibet ever does regain its autonomy, he will return to Tibet as a private citizen.

He also continues to write. Since his first book was published in 1962, he has authored more than sixty books, focusing primarily on Buddhism, compassion, and learning to live a happy life. His second autobiography, *Freedom in Exile: The Autobiography of the Dalai Lama*, was published in 1990, which updated the first account of his life. Other titles include *Four Essential Buddhist Commentaries* (1982), *A Human Approach to World Peace* (1984), *Transcendent Wisdom: A Commentary on the Ninth Chapter of Shantidera's Guide to the Bodhisattva Way of Life* (1988), *My Tibet* (1990), *Dimensions of Spirituality* (1995), *Healing Anger: The Power of Patience from a Buddhist Perspective* (1997), *The Joy of Living and Dying in Peace* (1997), *Ethics for the New Millennium* (1999), and *An Open Heart: Practicing Compassion in Everyday Life* (2001).

The future of the Dalai Lamaship is uncertain. If the country never re-turns to autonomy and China continues its strong hold, which is alto-gether likely, the Dalai Lama says that his reincarnation will be found outside Tibet for the first time in history. With more than 100,000 Ti-betans living in exile today, that prospect is conceivable. However, there may not be another Dalai Lama if the present Dalai Lama so wishes. It is his desire for a democratic Tibetan government, be it in Tibet or in exile. He sees his role as archaic and counterproductive to life in a modern world. As the Dalai Lama incarnates himself only when and where he wants to, lack of a proper candidate is feasible.

Yet a third high lama has possibilities, and the Tibetan people still look for a father figure. The Karmapa, head of the Kagyu School and third in line of high lamas following the Panchen Lama, recently escaped Tibet at age fif-teen. Will he be the new temporal and spiritual ruler of the Tibetans in exile? Or will a new Dalai Lama be born to assume the ancient birthright? Perhaps Tenzin Gyatso will feel that his work in strengthening his people for self-rule was not complete. Only time will tell whether he will choose to return to earth or to continue his existence in the Honorable Fields.

NOTES

1. Quoted in Howard C. Cutler, "The Mindful Monk," *Psychology Today*, May/June 2000, p. 34.

2. "The Dalai Lama's Biography," 9 September 1997, www.tibet.com.

3. Dalai Lama, "Human Rights and Universal Responsibility," Speech to United Nations World Conference on Human Rights, Vienna, 15 August 1993, www.freetibet.org/info/file6.htm.

4. Chris Colin, "The Dalai Lama," *Salon.com*, 28 November 2000, www.salon.com/people/bc/2000/11/28/dalai/index.html.

5. Dalai Lama, "Letter to President Bush," 12 September 2001, http://web.mit.edu/cms/reconstructions/expressions/dalai.html.

6. "Dalai Lama Says US War on Afghanistan is 'civilized,'" quoted in the Hindustan *Times* (l'Agence France-Presse), 24 October 2001, www.hindustan-times. com/nonfram/241001/dLAME58.asp.

7. Murray Bodo, O.F.M., "The Dalai Lama Visits Gethsemani," *Catholic Mes-senger*, January 1997, www.americancatholic.org/Messenger/Jan1997/feature1.asp.

8. "Statement of the Dalai Lama on the Demise of Mother Theresa," World Tibet Network News, 6 September 1997, www.tibet.ca/wtnarchive/1997/9/6 _1.html.

9. Hansard Parliamentary Debates for 27 April 1995, Stationery Office of the United Kingdom, www.parliament.the-stationery-office.co.uk/pa/cm199495/cmhansrd/1995–04–27/Debate-3.html.

10. Catronia Bass, "The Dalai Lama and the Playwright," *New Internationalist,* September 1990, www.oneworld.org/ni/issue211/lama.htm.

11. William Clinton, News Conference with President Jiang Zemin held in Beijing 27 June 1998, www.zpub.com/un/china27.html.

12. The Dalai Lama's Biography, Government of Tibet in Exile, www.tibet.com/DL/biography.html.

13. Colin, "The Dalai Lama."

14. "The Dalai Lama Discusses Science and Spirituality," interview by Larry King, *Larry King Live,* CNN, 26 June 2000, www.cnn.com/transcripts/006/26/lkl.oo.html.

15. Quoted in Jeff Greenwald, "Beam Me Up Dalai," *Salon.com,* www.salon.com/feb97/21st/startrek970227.html.

GLOSSARY

Ahimsa—Hindu and Buddhist doctrine of nonviolence

Amban—Chinese representative

Bardo—the spiritual state between death and reincarnation

Bodhisattvas—those who have attained spiritual Nirvana, but choose to return to Earth to help others reach enlightenment

Buddhahood—the state of spiritual enlightenment

Butter lamps—bowls of rancid butter into which a wick is set; a symbol of clarity

Chang—Tibetan beer

Chorten—dome-shaped structure, used as a Buddhist shrine, also known as a stupa

Chubas—kimono-like robes worn by both men and women

Damaru—small ritual drum

Dharma—holy teachings of Buddha

Dzomo—animals crossbred from yaks and cows

Dzong—fort

Geshe—Doctor of Metaphysics

Kalachakra Ceremony—rite wherein a sacred Mandala or sand painting is constructed and deconstructed to promote individual and world peace and physical balance

Kang—hollow, raised sleeping area made of clay brick, filled with dry grass and sand, usually lit for warmth

Karmapa—third highest lama in Tibet

Karmas—causes and effects

Kashag—the Dalai Lama's Cabinet

Kata—ceremonial scarf

Mandala—circular geometric design that symbolizes the universe in Buddhist and Hindu tradition

Mantra—verbally repeated prayer

Mendel Tensum—triple offering of reverence and homage

Momos—meat dumplings

Nirvana—in Buddhism, liberation from bondage of the human form or "the Wheel of Life"

Nyohogs—additional workers during sowing and harvesting season

Palanquin—a covered litter carried on the shoulders of four or more bearers

Panchen Lama—the second most important lama in Tibet

Patu—Lhasa woman's headdress

Rinpoché—title of respect, meaning "precious one"

Rosaries—strings of beads on which prayers are counted

Suzerainty—area where a stronger power holds dominion over the local government

Thukpa—soup made with thick millet noodles

Treljam—carriage or palanquin hung on two poles carried on the backs of mules

Tsampa—roasted barley meal, a staple in the Tibetan diet

Tulkus—spirits able to choose the time and place of their reincarnation

Yak butter tea—drink of black tea leaves and butter made from the milk of yaks

Yuleg—regular farm worker

SELECTION OF PUBLISHED WORKS BY THE FOURTEENTH DALAI LAMA

My Land and My People. New York: McGraw, 1962. Reprint, New York: Warner Books, 1997.

An Introduction to Buddhism. New Delhi: Tibet House, 1965.

The Opening of the Wisdom-Eye and the History of the Advancement of the Buddhadharma in Tibet. Bangkok: Social Science Association Press of Thailand, 1968.

Happiness, Karma, and Mind. Bloomington, Ind.: Tibet Society, 1969.

The Buddhism of Tibet and the Key to the Middle Way. Translated by Jeffrey Hopkins and Lati Rinpoché. New York: Harper, 1975.

Universal Responsibility and the Good Heart: The Message of His Holiness the XIV Dalai Lama of Tibet on His First Visit to the West in 1973. Dharamsala, India: Library of Tibetan Works and Archives, 1976.

Four Essential Buddhist Commentaries. Dharamsala, India: Library of Tibetan Works and Archives, 1982.

Kindness, Clarity, and Insight. Translated by Jeffrey Hopkins, edited by Jeffrey Hopkins and Elizabeth Napper. New York: Snow Lion Publications, 1984.

Opening the Eye of New Awareness. Translated by Donald S. Lopez, Jr., with Jeffrey Hopkins. Somerville, Mass.: Wisdom Publications, 1985.

Transcendent Wisdom: A Commentary on the Ninth Chapter of Shantideva's Guide to the Bodhisattva Way of Life. Translated, edited, and annotated by B. Alan Wallace. New York: Snow Lion Publications, 1988.

Freedom in Exile: The Autobiography of the Dalai Lama. New York: HarperCollins, 1990.

My Tibet. Berkeley: University of California Press, 1990.

Cultivating Daily Meditation. Dharamsala, India: Library of Tibetan Works and Archives, 1991.

The Way to Freedom, Core Teachings of Tibetan Buddhism. San Francisco: Harper-Collins, 1994.

The World of Tibetan Buddhism: An Overview of Its Philosophy and Practice. Translated by Geshe Thupten Jinpa. Somerville, Mass.: Wisdom Publications, 1995.

Beyond Dogma: Dialogues and Discourse. Translated by Alison Anderson, edited by Marianne Dresser. Berkeley, Calif.: North Atlantic Books, 1996.

The Wisdom Teachings of the Dalai Lama. New York: Plume, 1997.

Spiritual Advice for Buddhists and Christians, with Donald W. Mitchell and Dalai Lama Bstan-dzin-rgya-mtsho. London: Continuum, 1998.

Ethics for the New Millennium. New York: Riverhead, 1999.

Transforming the Mind. Edited by Geshe Thupten Jinpa. London: Thorsons Publications, 2000.

In My Own Words. Compiled by Mary Craig. London: Hodder and Stoughton, 2001.

An Open Heart: Practicing Compassion in Everyday Life. Edited by Nicholas Vreeland. New York: Little, Brown, 2001.

The Compassionate Life. Somerville, Mass.: Wisdom Publications, 2001.

The Dalai Lama's Book of Love and Compassion. London: Thorsons Publications, 2002.

SELECTED BIBLIOGRAPHY

BOOKS

Barber, Noel. *From the Land of Lost Content: The Dalai Lama's Fight for Tibet.* Boston: Houghton Mifflin, 1970.

Bell, Sir Charles. *Portrait of a Dalai Lama: The Life and Times of the Great Thirteenth.* 1946. Reprint, London: Wisdom Publications, 1987.

Chan, Victor. *Tibet Handbook: A Pilgrimage Guide.* Chico, Calif.: Moon Publications, 1994.

Farrer-Halls, Gill. *The World of the Dalai Lama: An Inside Look at His Life, His People, and His Vision.* Wheaton, Ill: Theosophical Publishing House, 1998.

Goldstein, Melvyn C. *The Snow Lion and the Dragon.* Berkeley: University of California Press, 1997.

Haw, Stephen G. *A Traveller's History of China.* Brooklyn: Interlink Books, 1997.

Holdich, Col. Sir Thomas H. *Tibet the Mysterious.* New York: Frederick Stokes, 1906.

Ngapo Ngwang Jigmei et al. *Tibet.* New York: McGraw-Hill, 1981.

Rinchen Lhamo. *We Tibetans.* Philadelphia: J.B. Lippincott Company, 1926.

Roberts, J. A. G. *A Concise History of China.* Cambridge, Mass.: Harvard University Press, 1999.

Snellgrove, David, and Hugh Richardson. *A Cultural History of Tibet.* New York: Praeger, 1968.

Tashai, Tsering, Melvyn Goldstein, and William Siebenschuh. *The Struggle for Modern Tibet: The Autobiography of Tashi Tsering.* Armonk, N.Y.: M.E. Sharpe, 1997.

PERIODICALS

Ahmedullah, Mohammed. "Marketing the Buddhist Message." *Bulletin of the Atomic Scientists*, March 2000, 13.

Cutler, Howard C. "The Mindful Monk." *Psychology Today*, May/June 2001, 34–38.

Dalai Lama. "His Journey: Exile Driven from His Homeland, Tibet's God-King Still Dreams of Marxism and Reconciliation." *Time*, October 1999, 78.

———. "China Must Keep Its Promise to Tibet." Washington *Post*, 22 May 2001, A21.

The Economist (U.S.). "A Break for Tibet." 14 November 1998, 22.

Goldstein, Melvyn C. "The Dalai Lama's Dilemma." *Foreign Affairs*, January–February 1998, 83–97.

Hindustan Times. "Dalai Lama Says US War on Afghanistan is 'Civilized.'" 24 October 2001.

Hundley, Helen. "Tibet's Part in the 'Great Game.'" *History Today*, October 1993, 45–50.

Iyer, Pico. "The God in Exile." *Time Australia*, 12 January 1998.

Kirkpatrick, David. "Buddhist to Businesses: Don't Ignore Tibet's Exiled Leaders." *Fortune*, 4 September 2000, 52.

Kolas, Ashild. "Tibet and the Politics of History." *Nordic Newsletter of Asian Studies*, July 1995.

Kuleshov, Nikolai S. "The Tibet Policies of Britain and Russia, 1900–14." *Asian Affairs*, February 2000, 41–48.

Kyabje Gelek Rinpoché and Robert A. F. Thurman. "Life in Old Tibet." *Civilization*, December 1999/January 2000, 65.

Liu, Melinda; Tony Clifton, Patricia Roberts and Thomas Laird. "A Secret War on the Roof of the World." *Newsweek*, 16 August 1999, 34–35.

Mathiassen, Charlotte. "Mythos Tibet." *Nordic Newsletter of Asian Studies*, June 1996.

Mazumdar, Sudip, and Melinda Liu. "The Politics of Reincarnation." *Newsweek International*, 6 March 2000, 28.

Mufson, Steven. "Bush Meets with the Dalai Lama." *Washington Post*, 24 May 2001, A15.

Nattier, Jan, and Robert A. F. Thurman. "Why Buddhism, Why Now?" *Civilization*, December 1999/January 2000, 67–68.

O'Donnell, Lynne. "Dalai Lama Faces Great Wall of Chinese Indifference." *Australian*, 31 January 2001, 7.

Rockhill, W. Woodville. "An American in Tibet: An Account of a Journey through an Unknown Land." *Century Magazine*, November 1890, 1+.

Schell, Orville. "Searching for the Dalai Lama." *Nation*, 3 April 2000, 18–21.

Simons, Lewis M. "The Strange Journey of Heinrich Harrer." *Smithsonian*, October 1997, 134–145.

Spaeth, Anthony. "Tempest in a Golden Urn: Under Beijing's Eye, Tibetan Monks Name a Panchen Lama to Rival the Dalai Lama's Choice." *Time*, 11 December 1995, 63.

Stanmeyer, Anastasia. "The Dalai Lama: Spiritual and Political Leader of 6 Million Tibetans." *Tampa Tribune*, 1992.

———. "No Dallying for the Dalai." 21 May 1994, 39.

———. "Tragedy on the Roof of the World: Tibet." 29 August 1998, 41–42.

Thurman, Robert. "The Long Road Home." *Civilization*, December 1999/January 2000, 70.

———. "A Lama to the Globe: The Dalai Lama Looks Beyond Tibet, and Meditates on His Reincarnation as an Ambassador of Buddhism." *Newsweek*, 16 August 1999, 32.

Woodward, Kenneth. "A Scratch in the Teflon Lama: A Rift over a Buddhist Deity Reveals That the Tibetan Religion Isn't Such a Shangri-La After All." *Newsweek*, 11 May 1998, 64–65.

Xinhua News Agency. "Dalai Lama Has Fooled Us." 25 April 2001.

———. "Tibetan Delegation in Sweden Discloses Dalai Lama's Conspiracy." 6 April 2001.

———. "Tibetan Eminent Monks Doubt Dalai Lama's Status as 'Religious Leader.'" 15 May 2001.

DOCUMENTS

Foreign Relations of the United States, 1964–1968, Vol. XXX, China.

United Kingdom. "The Anglo-Russian Entente." *Parliamentary Papers*, vol. 125, Cmd. 3750, 1907. www.lib.byu.edu/~rdh/wwi/1914m/anglruss.html.

United Nations General Assembly. *Resolution 1353 (XIV)*. 1959. http://www.tibet.com/Resolution/un59.html.

U.S. Department of State. *Testimony by Kent M. Wiedemann, Deputy Assistant Secretary of State for East Asian and Pacific Affairs Before Subcommittee on East Asian and Pacific Affairs*. Senate Foreign Relations Committee, 7 September 1995. http://dosfan.lib.uic.edu/ERC/bureaus/eap/950725WiedemannUSChina.html

INTERNET SOURCES

Amnesty International On-line. www.web.amnesty.org.

Christensen, John. "The Dalai Lama: Man of Peace Takes His Place on World Stage." *CNN Interactive, CNN In-depth Specials—Visions of China—Profiles: The Dalai Lama*, 1999. www.cnn.com/SPECIALS/1999/china.50/inside.china /profiles/dalai.lama.

Colin, Chris. "The Dalai Lama." *Salon.com*, 28 November 2000. www.salon.com.

Free the Panchen Lama Resource Center, 27 May 2001. www.tibet.ca/panchenlama.

Government of Tibet in Exile. www.tibet.com.

Greenwald, Jeff. "Beam Me Up Dalai." *Salon.com*, 27 February 1997. www.salon
.com.

Hitchens, Christopher. "His Material Highness." *Salon.com*, 13 July 1998.
www.salon.com.

International Committee of Lawyers for Tibet Reports. "The Case Concerning
Tibet: Tibet's Sovereignty and the Tibetan People's Right to Self-Determi-
nation." Tibet Justice Center, 1 June 1998. www.tibetjustice.org/reports
/sovereignty/index.html.

Snyder, Rachel Louise. "Laughing with the Dalai Lama." *Salon.com*, 5 October
1999. www.salon.com.

Stobdan, P. "Tibet and the Institution of Dalai Lama." Institute for Defence Studies
and Analyses, New Delhi, India. www.idsa-india.org/an-aug-5.html.

Tenzin Gyatso, the Dalai Lama. "China Must Keep Its Promise to Tibet."
Washingtonpost.com, 22 May 2001. www.washingtonpost.com.

Tibet Information Network. www.tibetinfo.net.

INDEX

About the Author

PATRICIA CRONIN MARCELLO is a freelance writer. She is the author of biographies of Jerry Garcia, Pope John Paul II, Princess Diana, and Matt Damon.